The Year of the Poet XII

May 2025

The Poetry Posse

inner child press, ltd.
'building bridges of cultural understanding'

The Poetry Posse 2025

Gail Weston Shazor
Shareef Abdur Rasheed
Teresa E. Gallion
hülya n. yılmaz
Noreen Snyder
Tzemin Ition Tsai
Elizabeth Esguerra Castillo
Jackie Davis Allen
Mutawaf Shaheed
Caroline 'Ceri' Nazareno
Ashok K. Bhargava
Alicja Maria Kuberska
Swapna Behera
Albert 'Infinite' Carrasco
Kimberly Burnham
Eliza Segiet
William S. Peters, Sr.

~ * ~

In order to maintain each poet's authentic voice, this volume has not undergone the scrutiny of editing. Please take time to indulge each contributor for their own creativity and aspirations to convey their uniqueness.

hülya n. yılmaz, Ph.D.
Director of Editing ~
Inner Child Press International

General Information

The Year of the Poet XII
May 2025 Edition

The Poetry Posse

1st Edition : 2025

This Publishing is protected under Copyright Law as a "Collection". All rights for all submissions are retained by the Individual Author and or Artist. No part of this Publishing may be Reproduced, Transferred in any manner without the prior **WRITTEN CONSENT** of the "Material Owners" or its Representative Inner Child Press. Any such violation infringes upon the Creative and Intellectual Property of the Owner pursuant to International and Federal Copyright Laws. Any queries pertaining to this "Collection" should be addressed to Publisher of Record.

Publisher Information
1st Edition : Inner Child Press
intouch@innerchildpress.com
www.innerchildpress.com

Copyright © 2025 : The Poetry Posse

ISBN-13 : 978-1-961498-65-5 (inner child press, ltd.)

$ 12.99

WHAT WOULD LIFE BE WITHOUT A LITTLE POETRY?

Dedication

This Book is dedicated to

Humanity, Peace & Poetry

the Power of the Pen

can effectuate change!

&

The Poetry Posse

past, present & future,

our Patrons and Readers &

the Spirit of our Everlasting Muse

*In the darkness of my life
I heard the music
I danced…
and the Light appeared
and I dance*

Janet P. Caldwell

Table of Contents

Foreword — *ix*

Preface — *xiii*

Emotions — *xv*

Resilience ~ Grief ~ Self Doubt

The Poetry Posse

Gail Weston Shazor	1
Alicja Maria Kuberska	7
Jackie Davis Allen	13
Tzemin Ition Tsai	21
Noreen Snyder	27
Elizabeth Esguerra Castillo	33
Mutawaf Shaheed	39
hülya n. yılmaz	49
Teresa E. Gallion	55
Ashok K. Bhargava	61
Caroline Nazareno-Gabis	69
Swapna Behera	75

Table of Contents ... *continued*

Albert Carassco	81
Kimberly Burnham	87
Eliza Segiet	95
William S. Peters, Sr.	101

May's Featured Poets — 107

Swayam Prashant	109
Ngozi Olivia Osuoha	115
Kazimierz Burnat	121
Deepak Kumar Dey	127

Inner Child Press News — 137

Other Anthological Works — 181

Foreword

Empathy in literature

I would like to draw attention to a topic that is not only close to my heart but is also fundamental to our human experience - empathy. Empathy, the ability to understand and share the feelings of another, is often described as the cornerstone of human connection. It is the bridge that allows us truly to connect with one another on a deeply emotional level. In a world that seems to be increasingly divided by differences in opinion, belief, and experience, empathy reminds us that despite our differences, we all experience joy, pain, love, and loss in similar ways.

As a poet, I have always believed in the power of words to evoke emotion, to spark understanding, and to inspire change. Through my poetry, I strive to create moments of connection, where the reader can step into another's shoes and see the world through their eyes. In literature, it's a bridge connecting the reader's heart with the characters' experiences. Through stories, we live countless lives, understanding emotions and situations far removed from our own. When we empathize with a character's plight, we're training our hearts to extend the same understanding to real people. But empathy is not just about understanding someone else's perspective; it is also about taking action. It is about using our understanding to guide our interactions with others, to treat them with kindness, compassion, and respect. One of the most beautiful aspects of empathy is its universality. It transcends language, culture, and ideology, binding us together in a shared experience of humanity. When we extend empathy to others, we not only enrich their lives but also our own.

Empathy is not always easy. It requires us to step outside of ourselves, to set aside our own preconceptions, and to truly listen to what others have to say. It requires courage and a willingness to be uncomfortable. But the rewards of empathy are great. It allows us to form deeper, more meaningful relationships, to foster a sense of belonging and community, and to create a world that is more just, compassionate, and understanding.

As we gather here today, in this beautiful city of Prague, let us recommit ourselves to the practice of empathy. Let us strive to see the humanity in one another, to listen with open hearts and minds, and to act with kindness and compassion. The poet Maya Angelou said:"I've learned that people will forget what you said, people will forget what you did, but people will never forget how you made them feel." Let us strive to make others feel seen, heard, and valued, for in doing so, we create a world that is more beautiful, more just, and more empathetic.

In conclusion, literature is not just an escape; it's a mirror reflecting our deepest capacity for empathy. It teaches and inspires us to extend our hand, understanding, and heart to others. Let's continue to read, not just for pleasure, but for empathy, for understanding, for a better world.

Alicja Maria Kuberska

Now Open for Submissions

innerchildpressanthologies@gmail.com

Preface

We, **Inner Child Press International, The Year of the Poet** and **The Poetry Posse** welcome you.

As we now are in our 12th year of monthly publications for **The Year of the Poet**, we continue to be excited.

This particular year we have chosen to feature a collection of human emotions. We do hope you enjoy the poet's perspectives on these subjects. Read ~ Learn.

For those of you who are not familiar with our story, back in 2013, a few of us poets got together with the simple intention of producing a book a month. That was our challenge. Since that time the enterprise has blossomed and brought forth a fruit that seems to keep on growing as evidenced as we enter 2023.

Our purpose is simple. Through our lyrical words and verse, we not only wish to share our poetic works, but we also have the poetic naiveté to believe that we can assist in the growth of consciousness of the things that have an effect our collective humanity. Therefore, we welcome your readership. For more about what we are attempting to accomplish, have a look at our Publishing Web Site . . . www.innerchildpress.com. If you would like to

know a bit more about this particular endeavor please stop by for a visit at :
www.innerchildpress.com/the-year-of-the-poet

Over the years, Inner Child Press has been socially active to bring awareness and catalog through literature the things that have an impact upon our world and its inhabitants. We have solicited, produced, underwritten and published quite a few volumes to that end. For more insight you may wish to visit : www.innerchildpress.com/the-anthology-market. If you are a writer, poet, or activist, you would be advised to keep a eye out for upcoming volumes should you desire to participate. All readers are welcomed as well. Note, that there is a myriad of published volumes that are available as a FREE PDF download as well as available for purchase at affordable prices.

We at this time extend to you our well wishes for your own personal journey and hope that you consider including us as a travel companion.

Bless Up

Bill

William S. Peters, Sr.

Publisher
Inner Child Press International
www.innerchildpress.com

Resilience, Grief, Self-Doubt

Bittersweetness	Empathy	Sadness
Bittersweetness	Lillies	Sunflowers

Is there ever pure joy without a tinge of sadness, regret, or guilt? Is bittersweetness everywhere? This is the question posed by this month's poems. The three emotion prompts are: Bittersweetness - A mix of joy and sadness in memories; Empathy - Understanding and connecting with others' struggles; and Acceptance - Coming to terms with oneself and life's realities.

How should we process mixed emotions, when things are good but not perfect or things are terrible but some good comes out of the mess? Should we pretend as Jennifer Lee says in Holding It Together? "Pretend happiness, even for just a little while... Faking sanity, with this smile..., Acting is for the better, The only way to hold it all together..." Or is it better to tell the truth and see that nothing is only one thing and that our perspective and experience colors everything. See the beauty and the mess. See the reality of it all.

Should we ask ourselves not is it true or real but is it useful? Does it help anyone to hold a particular belief or way of being too tightly? Can we accept the reality of what we see in front of us with the conflicting edges, as Coral Rumble says about Alzheimer's in My Name? "Grandma says she knows my name, just not at the moment when I came to see her, but she hasn't lied, I know my name is locked inside." We are lucky when we have our parents and grandparents well into adulthood but sometimes there is fear and sadness as we see them and ourselves age.

Do we as Maggie Smith says in Good Bones, make the best of what our life is? "I am trying to sell them the world. Any decent realtor, walking you through a real s-hole, chirps on about good bones: This place could be beautiful, right? You could make this place beautiful."

Ralph Waldo Emerson once wrote that if the stars came out only one night in a thousand years, that night would be considered an astounding spectacle, a wonder of the world, and anyone alive would stay up and behold them in breathless awe — and yet, there they are each cloudless night, no less miraculous for being so frequently visible.

What do you see in your life that is worthy of breathless awe?

Kimberly Burnham
Spokane Washington

Poets . . .
sowing seeds in the
Conscious Garden of Life,
that those who have yet to come
may enjoy the Flowers.

Poets, Writers . . . know that we are the enchanting magicians that nourishes the seeds of dreams and thoughts . . . it is our words that entice the hearts and minds of others to believe there is something grand about the possibilities that life has to offer and our words tease it forth into action . . . for you are the Poet, the Writer to whom the Gift of Words has been entrusted . . .

~ wsp

Poetry succeeds where instruction fails.

~ wsp

Coming Soon . . .

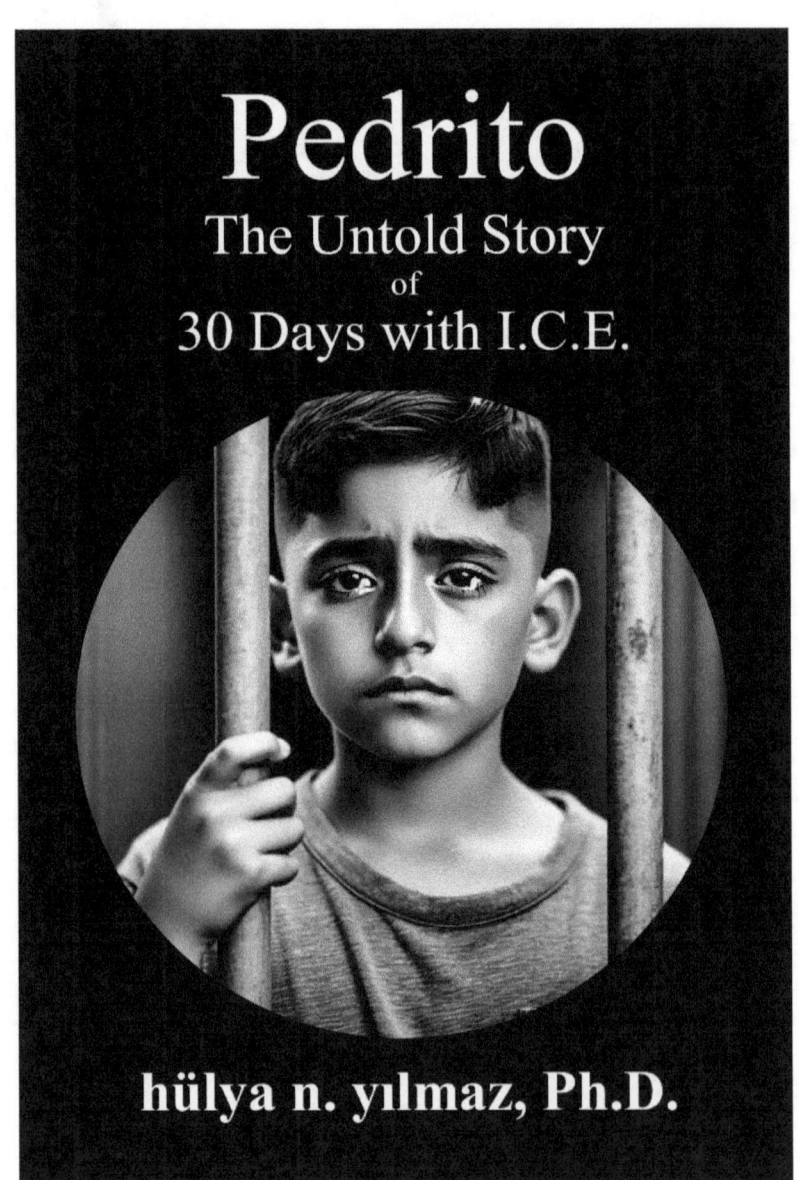

Gail Weston Shazor

Gail Weston Shazor

Gail Weston Shazor is a lover of words. She is fond of the arcane, unusual and the not yet words.

Coining words at an early age, there was often a bit of trouble with teachers, but she always had her mother and aunt to back up her choices in expression. Born in Mississippi, she spent her early years with her grandparents. Each of the four left very careful influences on her pre-schooling. She learned in turn how women worked in and out of the home and how men worked in and out of the home to support the family. She learned that a lack of proper schooling was not the only way to learn and understanding life was a great teacher. As in most rural families of color, women had a greater chance of formal learning. Both of Gail's grandmothers read out loud to the family whether it was the bible or the newspapers and important documents to their spouses.

Gail Weston Shazor has authored (so far) Notes from the Blue Roof, A Overstanding of an Imperfect Love, HeartSongs and Lies My Grandfather's Told Me. The number of anthologies is too many to list with the premier accomplishment of one of the contributors to The Year of The Poet. Gail will always lend her ink to community projects and will purchase the books of fellow poets in the Inner Child Press family.

Pots

Feed me goodness
From the pocket of your apron
Make each cut with precision
And hollow a space for faith
I believe
That there is enough salt
Enough love for a plenty
So I will stretch my feet under your table
To wait
Until the sizzle comes
From behind smoke furls
I place my hands in my lap for
Long ago I learned that elbows belonged
In other spaces than the table
The rhythm of pots and spoons
Soothe me
Your flavors are beautiful to watch
You move around the space
Of creation's hearth and even
When served hot or cold
In each of its order
My belly is satisfied
And my heart is full

Letters to my Muse
For Kit Shye Marlow

The closeness of your skin comforts me
You honor my quiet with one of your own
Keeping my words attached to
The paper as my paper
Must be contained in notebooks
You free my mind
To wander across worlds and return
With arms of letters
I use some and then
Save the others for you
For creativity breeds and nothing is useless
Letters
Comfort
I find this in your space
And the graciousness of your breath
I imagine how this will sound
When I speak them to you at their birth
When they are ready to be heard
Until then you nurture them with kisses
Unexpected kisses
Welcomed kisses
One day the letters in my heart
Will come forth
And you will know that I too
Love you.

Mothers

Spicy tomato apple reds
Beside cool greens
Bronzes and golds with blues
In between
Black and white and earth strong browns
This is the color of our queens
Her lips purse into small smiles
As the music sings her blurs
This is her vibration
Mother sun and daughter moon
Rock that baby bye
In a knowing of everything life
And easy as a Sunday afternoon
We are birthing colors
Hands clasped to share the power
Vibrating in drums and the
Siilvery metallicism of the winds
A circle of beginning and endings
In drumbeat of the woman

Alicja Maria Kuberska

Alicja Maria Kuberska

Alicja Maria Kuberska – awarded Polish poetess, novelist, journalist, editor.

She is a member of the Polish Writers Associations in Warsaw, Poland and IWA Bogdani, Albania. She is also a member of directors' board of Soflay Literature Foundation, Our Poetry Archive (India) and Cultural Ambassador for Poland (Inner Child Press, USA)

Her poems have been published in numerous anthologies and magazines in : Poland, Czech Republic, Slovakia, Hungary,Ukraina, Belgium, Bulgaria, Albania, Spain, the UK, Italy, the USA, Canada, the UK, Argentina, Chile, Peru, Israel, Turkey, India, Uzbekistan, South Korea, Taiwan, China, Australia, South Africa, Zambia, Nigeria

She received two medals - the Nosside UNESCO Competition in Italy (2015) and European Academy of Science Arts and Letters in France (2017). Ahe also received a reward of international literary competition in Italy ,, Tra le parole e 'elfinito" (2018). She was announced a poet of the 2017 year by Soflay Literature Foundation (2018).She also received : Bolesław Prus Prize Poland (2019), Culture Animator Poland (2019) and first prize Premio Internazionale di Poesia Poseidonia- Paestrum Italy (2019).

Alicja Maria Kuberska

Bittersweet

Joy and sorrow—
bound together for centuries,
sway gently on the same
swing of feelings.
Joy disappears
when sorrow soars,
but as it descends,
joy rises high
and fills the air with laughter.
Up—down, up—down,
for centuries the swing creaks,
refusing to stop.
It knows that stillness
would let nothingness devour
both laughter and tears.
Then the heart turns hollow,
like a deafened bell
suspended
between bittersweet thoughts.

Empathy

"Don't tear a butterfly's wings,"
my mother said—
"it won't fly,
and the pain is real.
Can't you see how much it fears you?"
I remember the insect
from my childhood—
a burst of colour,
a fleeting beauty,
taking flight from my palm.
Later I came to know pain,
when a drop of blood
bloomed on my finger
and a rainbow shimmered
through tear-filled eyes.
The world shared its feelings with me.
Now, sorrow and injustice weigh heavy,
while another's joy lifts me into the sky.
To understand,
to touch a thought,
to feel,
to open heart and mind wide—
to enter the soul of another—
that is what my mother taught me.

Alicja Maria Kuberska

Meta

Once I learned a truth of life—
Better is the enemy of good.
I know how hard it is to stop,
to abandon the endless chase
for one more dream.
Colourful ads coax us to consume:
"This shade is in this season—
throw away your old jeans,
your faded blouse.
Only violet suits the violet world!"
But I don't like violet—
it speaks of sorrow and mourning.
I prefer last year's blues and greens—
they bring peace and joy,
like a sunny sky,
or the first leaves of a birch.
To accept yourself
is to find delight
in every passing moment,
to wear what you love—
fashion be damned—
to look into the mirror with courage
and step out of the race
for nothing at all.

Jackie Davis Allen

Jackie Davis Allen

Jackie Davis Allen, otherwise known as Jacqueline D. Allen or Jackie Allen, grew up in the Cumberland Mountains of Appalachia. As the next eldest daughter of a coal miner father and a stay at home mother, she was the first in her family to attend and graduate from college. Her siblings, in their own right, are accomplished, though she is the only one, to date, that has discovered the gift of writing.

Graduating from Radford University, with a Bachelor's of Science degree in Early Education, she taught in both public and private schools. For over a decade she taught private art classes to children both in her home and at a local Art and Framing Shop where she also sold her original soft sculptured Victorian dolls and original christening gowns.

She resides in northern Virginia with her husband, taking much needed get-aways to their mountain home near the Blue Ridge Mountains, a place that evokes memories of days spent growing up in the Appalachian Mountains.

A lover of hats, she has worn many. Following marriage to her college sweetheart, and as wife, mother, grandmother, teacher, tutor, artist, writer, poet and crafter, she is a lover of art and antiques, surrounding herself, always, with books, seeking to learn more.

In 2015 she authored *Looking for Rainbows, Poetry, Prose and Art*, and in 2017, *Dark Side of the Moon*. Both books of mostly narrative poetry were published by Inner Child Press and were edited by hulya n. yilmaz in 2019, *No Illusions. Through the Looking Glass*, which was nominated to be considered for a Pulitzer Prize by the publisher and editor of Inner Child Press, ltd.

http://www.innerchildpress.com/jackie-davis-allen.php
jackiedavisallen.com

Jackie Davis Allen

Bittersweet

Reluctantly, I acquiesced.

Shy, with my mother's prodding,
Her encouragement, I told him, "Yes.
I will go to the prom with you tonight."

I was more nervous than excited.

Had ever two words passed
between us? An "Excuse-me"
as we filed out of Algebra II class?

Unlikely.

But here I am, four hours,
Into the acceptance, fear mounting.
My first Prom, my mother giddy.

As if she were attending! Not me!

Fortunately, with the steam iron
At the ready, a silken ball gown,
Pressed into its beauty, I slip into it.

Its elegant shape enhances mine.

No coquettish quips at my disposal,
Whatever will we talk about?
Why did I say yes to either of them?

I pull up my long white gloves.

My mother smoothes a stray wisp,
Of my bouffant hair, back into place.
A pause. Then a photo to memorialize.

"You'll be happy to see this one day."

Bittersweet, the memory
It has since become. And yet, time
erases the adolescent pain.

I'm remembering my Wallflower personae;

Abandoned by my Prince Charming,
My dancing shoes unused,
The truth of the age now reveals that

Which I wasn't able, then, to access.

Empathy

Sometimes,
Sometimes unknowingly,
Empathy is extended
By a smile, a hug, a card, a gift.
As a "just because", without any reason.
Without the giver having any idea
Of the greater significance to the recipient.

Feelings, emotions, are often hidden.

Words are not always needed, or
Voluntarily forthcoming, perchance due
To sorrow, sadness, depression, loss.
Perhaps a desire not to share for fear
Of appearing to boast, brag, or self-promote?
Acts of kindness express heart's gift
Of love and affection, interdependent
Of the need of the giver "to know".

Situations are not always shared.

Sometimes, what we say or do, expresses an
Empathy that lifts the spirit of a stranger, or
Someone we know slightly, friend or foe;
A family member or co-worker, without our
Having any idea how much it is needed.
We don't always know if our kindness
Has made a difference. Just remember:

We are all in need of empathetic care.

Acceptance

It happened, unintentionally.
I had the best of intentions in mind,
Something to please my mother,
Her party dress, freshly ironed.

While she was visiting next door.

As an adolescent, unknowingly,
The iron setting too hot,
A sizzling sound, a burning, gaping
Wound tragically opening up the bodice.

The scent was as horrific as the scene.

Tears abundant, plentiful
Though they were, nothing able
To turn back the clock of my mistake.
No way to erase my mothers anguish.

Her silence, the shock, it was unbearable.

 Apologies made, insufficient, I wept.
I begged, pleaded, ignorance. Ready
To accept penalty for my guilt, my offense.
My Momma just selected another dress to wear.

She never mentioned it to me. Ever.

Jackie Davis Allen

Tzemin Ition Tsai

Tzemim Ition Tsai

Dr. Tzemin Ition Tsai comes from the Republic of China(Taiwan). In addition to being a professor of literature at a university, he is more committed to writing poems, novels, and proses. He is also an editor of "Reading, Writing and Teaching" academic text, an International editor of "Contemporary dialogues" literary periodical in Macedonia, and Vice-Chairman of the International Jury of the SAHITTO INTERNATIONAL AWARD in Bangladesh, and a columnist for "Chinese Language Monthly" in Taiwan.

In a wide range of literary creations, he is particularly fond of interesting stories or novels, and writing articles or poems about the feelings of nature and human beings. He has won many national literary awards. His literary works have been anthologized and published in books, journals, and newspapers in more than 55 countries and have been translated into more than 24 languages.

The Memory of Water, the Silent Flower

Water never knocks; it simply gathers quietly behind the door,
Like a cup of thoughts left uncollected from last night.
Moonlight passes over, leaving fingerprints of tranquil ripples.
You ask, is it a tide?
I say, no, it is the wave that once embraced the shore,
Only to retreat, leaving behind a ring of sand and an empty chair.
Not every drop of water will flow from the eyes;
Some, along the walls of the heart,
Slowly seep,
Silently carving the layers of time's rock.
We learn to hold water, learn to evaporate,
Learn to say "I'm fine" in the crowd,
Like learning to grow a flower in a broken cup
That needs no rain.
This flower has no name, no fragrance,
But it remembers the language of the clouds,
And knows that the riverbed inside you has never dried.
Water is the plant of time,
Needing neither sunlight nor roots,
It sprouts through memory,
And bears fruit through silence.

The Slant of Time, Covering the Misspelled Name

Before ink meets the page,
you believe yourself a mountain—
but once the stroke is drawn,
you are only a trembling line of river.
A name, once written, feels like a borrowed fate,
yet always misread, misspelled, mistaken.
Time offers no corrections,
only the silence
as you revise yourself again and again.
Your true name is not in any registry,
but in the wrinkled scrap you almost threw away.
Some write dynasties across lifetimes,
others, doubt themselves
in the fine brushstrokes of marginal script.
"Too light? Too heavy? Not me enough?"
You think setting down the pen is the end—
but Time,
it draws a slanted line across your page.
Not to erase,
but to leave space for you to write again.

Above the Folds, a Faintly Visible Route

We were all once paper—
white, fragile, spread open and folded by time.
At times, an unnamed hand folded us into a small boat,
drifting down the channels of childhood,
vanishing into the undercurrents called reality.
Yet some paper,
even when damp, torn, and marked by the lines of history,
chooses to unfold once more beneath the sun—
not to return to its original flatness,
but to allow each crease
to become a coordinate,
writing directions within the fragments.
These papers have learned not to yearn to be poetry,
but to quietly exist behind it,
like a map, for others to fold, unravel, lose their way, and rediscover.
Not every tear
needs mending—
some cracks are themselves a route, uncharted.

Noreen Snyder

Noreen Snyder

Noreen Ann Snyder has been writing since she was a teenager. She writes a variety of different topics. Her favorite poetic forms are Sonnets, Blitz, Haiku, Tanka, and Free Verse. She always learning different poetic forms.

Noreen Ann Snyder is a poet, writer, and an author of five books, (four books are co-authored with her late husband, Garry A. Snyder.) Her poetry is in several Inner Child Press Anthologies. She is the founder of The Poetry Club on Facebook.

Empathy Is...

When you meet someone,
whether it's at a store, a park,
a restaurant, or any other place;
greet them with a warm smile
and say, "Hello! How are you today?"
Let's spread some positivity
and make someone's day
a little brighter.
You don't know what he or she is
going through.
So let's be kind, gentle, loving,
understanding, and be a friend.
Show empathy
and let that person know
he or she is valued.

Acceptance

Concentrate on the present
not dwell on the past.
Accept who you are-
the good and the bad.
Some traits you cannot change
so accept it what it is.
You will find more inner peace,
accepting your choices you make,
deeper and rejuvenating sleep,
and less stress
not worrying so much
That's what acceptance is.

Best and Worst of Times

Best of times

were you and I together

missing those days.

Worst of times

when you are no longer

here with me.

Elizabeth E. Castillo

Elizabeth Esguerra Castillo

Elizabeth Esguerra Castillo is a multi-awarded and an Internationally-Published Contemporary Author/Poet and a Professional Writer / Creative Writer / Feature Writer / Journalist / Travel Writer from the Philippines. She has 2 published books, "Seasons of Emotions" (UK) and "Inner Reflections of the Muse", (USA). Elizabeth is also a co-author to more than 60 international anthologies in the USA, Canada, UK, Romania, India. She is a Contributing Editor of Inner Child Magazine, USA and an Advisory Board Member of Reflection Magazine, an international literary magazine. She is a member of the American Authors Association (AAA) and PEN International.

Web links:

Facebook Fan Page

https://free.facebook.com/ElizabethEsguerraCastillo

Google Plus

https://plus.google.com/u/0/+ElizabethCastillo

Elizabeth Esguerra Castillo

Empathy

In quiet moments, hearts can meet,
A bridge of kindness, soft and sweet.
When eyes connect, a story shared,
In silent whispers, souls laid bare.

A gentle touch, a knowing glance,
In shared burdens, we find our chance.
To hold each other, to understand,
We walk together, hand in hand.

A world that aches, divided so,
But empathy can help us grow.
With open hearts, we sift through pain,
And in our kindness, love will reign.

So let us listen, let us care,
For every struggle, we can bear.
In simple acts, our strength will rise,
A tapestry of shared goodbyes.

Shadow Dance

In the quiet of the evening glow,
Shadows dance on paths we used to know,
Laughter echoes through the gentle trees,
Whispers of time carried by the breeze.

Moments cherished, yet tinged with pain,
Softly falling like a summer rain,
Each smile painted with a touch of grey,
Bittersweet memories linger, come what may.

The warmth of embraces, now just a sigh,
Photographs faded, as seasons fly by,
Yet in these fragments, a treasure resides,
A tapestry woven where love never hides.

Though time may dim the spark we knew,
The heart holds fast to the joy and the blue,
In every heartbeat, in every tear,
Bittersweet memories forever near.

Elizabeth Esguerra Castillo

Echoes of the Past

In quiet corners of the mind,
Where echoes of the past unwind,
Memories dance like fading light,
In whispers soft, they take their flight.

A child's laughter in the breeze,
Chasing shadows, climbing trees,
Days of sun and endless play,
Captured moments, here to stay.

A photograph, a sunset hue,
Each glance a story, old yet new,
The scent of pine, the ocean's roar,
Remind us of what we adore.

Time may fade the colors bright,
But in our hearts, they burn alight,
For every joy, each tear we've shed,
Builds the tapestry that we thread.

So let us hold these treasures dear,
The smiles shared, the whispered cheer,
For in each memory, we find our way,
A light to guide us day by day.

Mutawaf Shaheed

Mutawaf Shaheed

C. E. Shy has been writing since the seventh grade. He continued writing through high school, until he became more involved in sports. After his graduation, he worked at the White Motors Company where he wrote for the company's newspaper. He started a column called: "The Poet's Corner." That was his first published work.

www.innerchildpress.com/c-e-shy.php

Mutawaf Shaheed

New Sensations

Is it your power or my
weakness that has me
longing for the new
sensations? Maybe it's
a combination of the
two?

I'm coming from the land
of giants just to visit who?
I didn't know what to expect,
I never thought it'd be you.

I find myself ignoring my
logic and submitting to
overwhelming whims.
They swim inside my head.
Then abide in where I
thought I'd find a safety valve.

As I come closer to the
edge of what I consider it, it
has me within it's grip. What
I did, slid through my mind
like a new sensation often does,
if one, can capture one.

Never sure about a mind set
that will survive the desire to
achieve something higher. I
can't be confident I'll be able
to escape my lower desires.

The Year of the Poet XII ~ May 2025

Unable to describe what they
are, Is a for another conversation.
For now, I remain subjugated to a
new sensation.

Mutawaf Shaheed

Delighted

Something about the candles light
Tonight, has it shining different than
the nights before. What hid in the
mist can't hide anymore. As I examine
the hours, I hear you laugh lightly, it
left me sort a smiling.

Lying here with you, I have come to
terms that there is only so much love
 we can give and take , we won't take
any of it with us. We weren't built that
way.

Keeping my imagination under control
makes my health a lot better. A cavalcade
of voices offer me choices, every now and
then there comes a visit from the common
cold.

Unable to hide from the things that abide
 inside me , I watch out for the stuff outside,
making sure they don't try to rusticate inside
and attempt to dominate me for any length
of time

Constantly improving on the technics, on
how to more effectively to block low blows.
Trying to guess what tests comes next?
There's less of a guess if you read the text,
where the answers come and go.

The Year of the Poet XII ~ May 2025

I see some entity using the clouds as a shroud,
they don't particularly care for me. What can be
salvaged from the ravages of time? The quicker we
come to the point of all this, the sooner we can
relax.

When eliminating the but, if, maybe, luck , chance,
understanding that sooner come before later,
knowing there is no need for a moderator, eliminates
any doubt, that has been used against us. Love is
situated in the middle.

What it means and how you feel is only real to those
who feel it. Can it mutate, if so into what? Left alone
to choose a champion never knowing what that means.
Not to worry, because everything with us is temporary…

Sorry, I didn't mean to drift, I am delighted to be here
with you again! These other things I would not dare share,
or whisper in your ear.

Mutawaf Shaheed

You and I

Paper plums and graphite trees ,
I did all of this for you and me.
I moved some ice bergs to our
favorite lake, so you and I could
share a little drink. I didn't know
our house would sink.

I changed the course of rivers, and
built some dams. Can't you see how
smart I am? My friend and me created
an income stream, by selling dreams
and make believe. By having many
tricks up our sleeves there's a lot of
things we achieved.

The rivers, we turned red white and
blue, sweetheart I did this for you!
I stole and tricked some folks from
other shores and brought them here
do your chores, to be my whores.

They had the nerve to think they'd be
free, the constitution never said that to
me. Well, I couldn't really read or write
good myself, So, I put that up on my shelf.
I knew I was right because I'm white. I'm
the cops and the robbers too.

Ain't anything the bleeding hearts can do.
The high court said that I could shoot them
too. Who do you know that could take my
place? My grand-dad and his old man, told
me, I was from a superior race. No need of a
high IQ, to do what I do.

The land I took is getting dryer by the day, what the Hell, is wasn't mine anyway. I'll be safe, as long as the negroes continue to pray to papier-mache,'you remember, that's the crap we sent their way.

I marvel at how stupid people can be! The stuff I do to them, and they still can't see, they sit there and hope I'll leave them alone. I sit and watch them and throw them another bone.

Mutawaf Shaheed

hülya n. yılmaz

hülya n. yılmaz

Liberal Arts Professor Emerita, hülya n. yılmaz [sic] is Co-Chair and Director of Editing Services at Inner Child Press International, a published author, ghostwriter, and translator (EN, DE, and TU; in any direction). Her literary contributions appeared in a large number of national and international anthologies.

hülya writes creatively to attain and nourish a comprehensive awareness for and development of our humanity.

hülya n. yılmaz, a traveler on the journey called "life" . . .

Writing Web Site
https://hulyanyilmaz.com/

Editing Web Site
https://hulyasfreelancing.com

having missed

several of their early ages,
sadness envelopes me today;
actually, many a day,
but then they both send me their pure love
out of the blue, and i notice
the sunshine as well as the clouds
alongside of which i am lifted
far above the ground

while i still take in the precious memories
of their unforgettable baby smells,
i feel thrilled to be able to hug
on this joyous day and beyond
my gorgeous grandchildren
of a lovely 10 and a lovely 8

Hypersensitive

It's not a self-diagnosis.
I have been told this fact many times.

The suffering of a living being
Gets me down every single time.

My sorrow does not disappear fast.
It lingers on and on. It just lasts.

"I'm an empath," some people say.
That much, I truly understand.
I, too, can say so out loud.
However, when the object is my self,
I act as if the self does not exist.
I act as were "hypersensitive" my only name.

exaggerating

we laugh and we cry
often, without asking "why"

we contemplate, and we comment
then react to the reactions of others

we like the "Like" and the "Love" choices
on social media's virtual realities

we get angry, even quite upset
when we see we haven't been read

we fail to pause and think legibly
about our futile attempts at popularity

we engage in arguments of no-end
with the countless trolls and bots

it's just so
that we exaggerate

Teresa E. Gallion

Teresa E. Gallion

Teresa E. Gallion is a seeker on a journey to work on unfolding spiritually in this present lifetime. Writing is a spiritual exercise for Teresa. Her passions are traveling the world and hiking the mountain and desert landscapes of the western United States. Her journeys into nature are nurtured by the Sufi poets Rumi and Hafiz. The land is sacred ground and her spiritual temple where she goes for quiet reflection and contemplation. She has published five books: Walking Sacred Ground, Contemplation in the High Desert, Chasing Light, a finalist in the 2013 New Mexico/Arizona Book Awards, Scent of Love, a finalist in the 2021 New Mexico/Arizona Book Awards and Come Egypt in 2024. She has two CDs, *On the Wings of the Wind* and *Poems from Chasing Light*. Her work has appeared in numerous journals and anthologies.

Website: http://teresagallion.yolasite.com/

The Pendulum

Joy and sadness are the pendulum we engage.
A balancing act that requires a learning curve.
It is a bittersweet embrace given to all souls.

Love enfolding and love loss,
a blend of sad and cherished moments
build our strength to keep on walking.

We can only learn and grow,
when we experience the highs and lows
driving the highway of life.

Wake up each morning
and massage your muscle memory.
It is waiting to expose you to the light.

Empathetic Maneuvers

A soft blanket lies on the ground
embracing your words and mine.
Eco's of joy massage your sorrows.
Sweet whispers raise your spirit.

We are entwined in the moment
that binds my heart to yours.
Beyond the veils and masks,
you feel the strength of my love.

My gentle touch is always there
bathing you with love and understanding.
Inhale the fragrant blooms around our blanket.
Embrace the compassion flowing to you.

Simple Act

She scatters words across the meadows
and whispers sweet notes to the grass.
Smiles bend like a wind-blown kiss.

This is not the first-time words
ran through the forest landscape.
Flowers enjoy that special touch too.

That is the beauty of acceptance.
Everything and every being
is touched by that simple act of love.

Ashok K. Bhargava

Ashok K. Bhargava

Ashok Bhargava is a poet, writer, inspirational speaker and a literary consultant. He has attended poetry conferences in Italy, Turkey, India and Philippines. His latest book "Riding the Tide" about his battle with cancer has been translated and published in Arabic, Hindi, Telugu and Bengali languages. He is a contributing writer to several anthologies worldwide including World Poetry Almanac 2014. He has been published in numerous print and online magazines.

Ashok has won many accolades including Poet Ambassador to Japan, Kalidasa International award, World Poetry Lifetime Achievement award, Writers Beyond Borders Peace award and Tapsilog Leadership award for his community involvement. He is founder of Writers International Network Canada Society to discover, nourish, recognize and celebrate writers, poets and artists and to assist them to network with the community at large. He is the author of eight books of poetry and one anthology. He is Artist-in-Residence at Moberly Arts & Cultural Centre and also co-edits the literary section of The Link Newspaper.

An Unwilling Prisoner of the Past

This feeling that something was missing made me despise myself – St. Augustine

I'd like to find her but I can't.

I feel I found her at times.
But then she is gone.

This bone-deep grief
cannot be fathomed.

It has been an ingrained
persistent
pain
if you can understand.

I remember that moment, in detail.
Am I all that has gone wrong
and all that has not. I have become
a prisoner of the past.

I see a figure
rising,
looking out at me
wanting to say nothing, or too much.
Evading and returning.

Does she not
like to be revealed
the one I took as my daughter.

She's gone and
she can't hear me
calling her back.

She never was, or it only
looks like that.

Ashok K. Bhargava

About New You

It's been so long since
I was at this spot and now I am back.

The water is flowing swiftly.
Deep coldness.

It makes me tremble and shiver.
It makes me cry and smile
at the impermanence of life.
To feel the current

you have to step down.
Its force will carry you
if you let it
though I don't know how far.

Brother, I scatter your remains here.
I look as it goes with the flow.

You have become someone entirely new -
a photograph hanging on the wall
a garland of flowers
a shadow of what you were once.

Tears tide inside me.
Only those who love know of it.

I wish you'd come back . . .

Morning Prayers

Out of the quarrel with others we make rhetoric;
out of the quarrel with ourselves we make poetry —
~ W.B. Yeats

Folded hands
rise with hazy breaths
become shapes on a windowpane.

They convert to teardrops and
flow down in streaks
as the sunrays embrace them.

Watery strips elevate my soul
make me flow gently
silently.

Hungry for a change
salivating for better seasons
I hold on.

Delays and frustrations
twists and turns
circumvent
changes to occur.

It was a monk, I learnt
who created the pretzel -
an acknowledgement to
our circular complexities.

Caroline 'Ceri Naz' Nazareno Gabis

Caroline 'Ceri' Nazareno-Gabis

Caroline 'Ceri Naz' Nazareno-Gabis, author of Velvet Passions of Calibrated Quarks, World Poetry Canada International Director to Philippines is a multi-awarded poet, editor, journalist, educator, peace and women's advocate. She believes that learning other's language and culture is a doorway to wisdom.

Among her poetic belts include **Gabrielle Galloni Memorial Panorama International Youth Award 2022**, Panorama Youth Literary Awards 2020, 7th Prize Winner in the 19th, 20th and 21st Italian Award of Literary Festival; Writers International Network-Canada ''Amazing Poet 2015'', The Frang Bardhi Literary Prize 2014 (Albania), Poet Journalist Award 2014 (Tuzla, Istanbul, Turkey) and World Poetry Empowered Poet 2013 (Vancouver, Canada). She's a featured member of Association of Women's Rights and Development (AWID), The Poetry Posse, Galaktika Poetike, Asia Pacific Writers and Translators (APWT), Axlepino and Anacbanua. Her poetry and children's stories have been featured in different anthologies and magazines worldwide.

Links to her works:

http://panitikan.ph/2018/03/30/caroline-nazareno-gabis/

https://apwriters.org/author/ceri_naz/

http://www.aveviajera.org/nacionesunidasdelasletras/id1181.html

Caroline 'Ceri' Nazareno-Gabis

The Paradox of Tears and Joy

As you bid adieu to the fleeting sun,
Moments dissolve to the fiery hue,
The touch of the whispering breeze,
Is an echo lingering like a gentle ache.

It's like love so sweet at full bloom,
But when the heart breaks its vows,
The tears flow in the river beds,
Somehow, eternal dreams are not ours.

Bittersweet threads, weaving day and night,
Sweet Lilies don't bear honeycombs for everyone,
Through tears that fall from a gloomy day,
Can be a triumph and joy for a mother who bear
A child in her womb,
To cherish a life,
And the celebration of a poignant journey.

The Empathy Force

A silent bridge is there

When you have nothing to say,

A heart that listens,

Is a soul in tune with the open field,

It gives light to a darkened room,

Or music to someone's doom,

To feel one's shoes and hear their fears,

To be happy in their joyous fame,

To see one's stormy veil off the ground,

Empathy yields as you mend the petals

Love takes root when shared like flowers.

The Gift of Acceptance

The current flow of a stream,

From the clear sky after the storm

Your feet stand on where paths must go,

Live it and carry your vision.

Acceptance is a steady art,

Carving caring minds and patient hands

To lift the stories: You Are Not Alone!

We etched a world of Love and Peace.

Swapna Behera

Swapna Behera

Swapna Behera is a trilingual poet, translator, environmentalist, editor from India and author of seven books of different genres including one on children's literature on Environment. She is the recipient of International UGADI AWARD 2019, honoured from Gujurat Sahitya Akademi 2022, 2021 International Poesis Award of Honor as Jury, Pentasi B World Fellow Poet, Honoured Poet of India from Seychelles Government and International awards from Algeria, Morocco, Kajhakhstan, modern Arabic Literary Renaissance of Egypt, International Arts Council Argentina etc. Her stories, poems, articles are published in many International and National magazines and ezines. Her poem A NIGHT IN THE REFUGEE CAMP is translated into 67 languages. She has received over 60 National and International Awards. At present she is the Cultural Ambassador for India and South Asia of Inner Child and the life member of Odisha Environmental Society

Email
swapna.behera@gmail.com

Web Site
http://swapnabehera.in/

Swapna Behera

either you get bitter or better

the birds twitter
have no concrete home
 never they go markets
they have two tiny wings to fly
that is all they have
they can make nests have their own language
they are the survivors
 who fly from Siberia to your zone in winter
they have no electronic gadgets
 to measure the distance or heights
you have everything you need
sometimes your accessories are precious than you
in the name of peace you create war ,
 kill and experiment on money time energy
do you have time to heal yourself
there is no time for you
you are the slave of yourself
 sitting in the global market
your identity is just a number
the human being within you is lost
you went to moon, space and sea
 in search of a better you
but the best of you is still singing
we have to make a team to delete all odium
and celebrate the coronation of love

Empathy vs Sympathy

along the lissom tide
 the smell of the news paper
the legacy of trees or villages
nakedness is a divine gift
sacrificing ego, superego
ruffled hair and those innocent eyes
sing the ecstasy
entering the zone of darkness
I know; each hemisphere has a new agenda
I know; each child has a story to tell
where is empathy?
the lady on the wheel chair needs empathy
an infrastructure to grow
certainly not a seminar lecture
or any power point data presentation
research scholars are moving around
the orphan boy is feeding the street dog
someone has thrown the biscuit packet from the running bus
now both are happy with broken biscuits
who has seen tomorrow?
every moment someone is crucified
every moment a tree is cut
a river dries up carrying loads of garbage
empathy with action has to be activated
sympathy is thematic
human race is marching forward
an unseen Heaven is smiling crossing every border

accepting a honeymoon

Jasmines spread on the bed
the bride with croquette gown
sits like a huge pumpkin
couple of months ago
the groom went to see the girl
Aha! Her pretty long hair with flowers curl
her smile was hotter than samosas on plate
eyes met and he smiled
the girl was happy for his teeth so white
must be too romantic
using branded tooth paste
since that day he had all dreams
to fore play with her hair on the first meet
on the dreamy night he raised her veil
Lo! Behold she is bald!!!
explained she, 'It is coz of typhoid''
he screamed with anger you a cheat!
 tongues twisted; his denture slipped
dreams broke like crispy golgappas
big in the glass box; sour when crashed
both faced opposite with tear and fear
the wig and denture slept hugging each other
accepting the honeymoon
with a song of jinga la la ......

(Samosa is an Indian snack)

Albert 'Infinite' Carrasco

Albert 'Infinite' Carassco

Albert "Infinite The Poet" Carrasco is an urban poet, mentor and public speaker.

Albert believes his experience of growing up in poverty, dealing with drugs and witnessing murder over and over were lessons learnt, in order to gain knowledge to teach. Albert's harsh reality and honesty is a powerfully packed punch delivered through rhyme. Infinite grew up in the east part of the Bronx and still resides there, so he knows many young men will follow the same dark path he followed looking for change. The life of crime should never be an option to being poor but it is, very often.

Infinite poetry @lulu.com

Alcarrasco2 on YouTube

Infinite the poet on reverbnation

Infinite Poetry

www.lulu.com/us/en/shop/al-infinite-carrasco/infinite-poetry/paperback/product-21040240.html

www.innerchildpress.com/albert-carrasco

Bittersweet Empathy Acceptance

I lived a life that would seem like a movie to others, I know if I could get on the big screen my nightmarish dream of reality would pack in cinemas, I can see it now "the life of and urban poet" under Tyler Perry's studio, Sony or Paramount pictures. It'll be bittersweet. A story of harsh and complicated trials and tribulations, actions and reactions of trying to end poverty by hustling on New York streets. Living a life of crime and witnessing destruction and flatlines was Lessons learned to be taught as education. Where I'm from monetary oppression runs rampant, which usually leads to drug traffic, drug habits, the penitentiary, cemeteries and the cause of insanity. I know the outside of the underworld would watch my life and the lives of many before and after me with empathy, I've been twenty years clean but my mind is still in recovery… I was strung out on misery, the ghetto was my company. I am the drug dealer you want your children to be around, I know I'll be granted acceptance by the masses due to my influence and lyrical substance on substances created by my thoughts manifested into sight and sound.

Memory

My memory amazes me, I can think of a point in time and remember people, places and conversations vividly. I can hear voices, my memory also has excellent sound quality. I can go back to an argument/debate and get the last word in, because in that memory their last word were their last words, so they're unable to respond. I can go back to good times to see smiles and laughter and repeat those times over and over, because I will never be able to see or hear those visions and sounds out of my head in the future. I can feel energy in my memories just as physical chemistry but mentally. I mean who ever is in my thought feels like they're amongst me, spiritually. I constantly reminisce about my sandbox brothers from another mother that passed from sickness, suicide and murder. I wish I had such powerful vision that I'll be able to see angels and hone in on hell on earth to heaven frequencies so I can hear and speak to them. If that was a possibility I wouldn't have to just rely on my fond memory, I'll just stop what I'm doing, tilt my head toward the sky, speak, look and listen.

Not just a rhyme

I don't just write rhymes, I write visions between lines, I spit experiences into mics, Where there's darkness, I am light, Outside hears me, Insiders read me via my published books or kites. Infinite is the epitome of my genre of urban poetry. I'm talking about poverty, trap, decades long sentences in the (pain)itentiary and Sunday trips to cemeteries to visit victims of the ultimate felony. I tell my story of my life in the game from the beginning to the end without glorification, I can't edit the truth because the ink in my pen is nonfiction. so when you read me or hear me writing or talking about how I was street dreaming, how I was in the kitchen whippn that Benjamin badder, how i had money on top of money, how I had sport cars with turbos and superchargers, how my neck hung with Lazarus, crucifix's and Santa Barbara's, how there was constant gunfights for control of red stained green paper… I'm doing so to get the attention of those trying to blow as well as those already cuttn and cookn blow because if you tell someone hungry for money that, that life can be theirs… that's all they need to know. That's a part of the truth. There are gains but the loses outweigh them. We dreamt together, we stood cheffn and baggn together, chains hung, we shun together, we got on highways and looked at rear view mirrors and saw a hazard light motorcade of japs and Germans purr'n together. One by one I carried all of them on my shoulder as a pallbearer. That's also the truth. That's the fuel to my fire and the reason why I meticulously organize letters adding pros and cons together, I've dealt with too many triple days of rain, so I teach the Ying and Yang of the game with my pain to change the futures weather.

Kimberly Burnham

Kimberly Burnham

A brain health expert (PhD in Integrative Medicine) and award-winning poet, Kimberly Burnham lives with her wife and family in Spokane, Washington. Kim speaks extensively on peace, brain health, and *"Awakenings: Peace Dictionary, Language and the Mind, a Daily Brain Health Program."* She recently published *"Heschel and King Marching to Montgomery A Jewish Guide to Judeo-Tamarian Imagery."* Currently work includes *"Call and Response To Maya Stein an Anthology of Wild Writing"* and a how-to non-fiction book, *"Using Ekphrastic Fiction Writing and Poetry to Create Interest and Promote Artists, Writers, and Poets."*

Follow her at https://amzn.to/4fcWnRB

Kimberly Burnham

On Waking in Portland

This morning,
I woke in my cousin's guest room
in a city not my own
but familiar now
like a coat I borrowed for a season

The clinic waits just down the road.
the work—still mine.
hands remembering what they've practiced
for thirty years
how to touch pain
and teach it to loosen its hold

I meant to retire.
I meant to sit longer with the trees
read more books
work in the garden
living the life of someone
with no appointments

But the world whispered
come back
so I did
and each day I learn more

Today I will tend
to another family.
for a moment,
bound by care

There will be progress.
a child's gait

smoother than yesterday,
a body more at ease in its skin.
changes that may outlast me
a gift I can still give

Still, I miss home
a six-hour drive away in Spokane
my wife. the hum of a quiet Spokane morning.
my desk waiting
with pen and paper

But joy lives here too—
in the practice,
the pride,
knowing that legacy
does not need a grand announcement.
sometimes, it is the simple, steady doing
of the thing you were meant to do

Home

No one leaves home
unless the heart insists.
unless the road rises up
and says come

Sometimes, we are lucky
we leave home because the world
has opened its arms to learning,
to longing, to the wild pull of adventure

We grow in the leaving.
our roots stretch
a seed blown away
but we carry an invisible thread
back to the place that held us
when we were small
and if love waits there
we are luckier still

No one leaves
unless something ahead glimmers
a job, a welcoming place with peace
or the promise of it
Even if the work is heavy
and no one else wants it

Even then we leave
home

No one leaves
a loving home
unless they experience
another kind of love
brave and vast.
the kind that wants to nest

If we are fortunate,
we land in a country
where that love is allowed
to stand in the daylight,
where the laws and culture see it
and say, Yes

But some are not so lucky.
falling in love
in the wrong place
at the wrong time
the wrong gender but still we leave home
in hope of a new place for love

No one leaves home
without the sky cracking open
or the earth shifting beneath our feet
we flee because bullets
have found the schoolyard
because the night is too loud
danger too near

And still we hope.
that the new place
will be quiet.
that the sky above it
will hold only stars not fire

That the door
will stay on its hinges,
that the word "home"
will not be rewritten
once again
in terror

Kimberly Burnham

The Woodpecker

Last night, I heard him
a presence, a rhythm deep in the trees,
drumming old wood for insects or simply
to say: I am here.

This morning appeared through the window
the Northern Flicker
noisy architect of spring

A red crescent
graced the back of his head,
a dark bib draped over his lungs
his body a canvas of speckled light —
all cream and ink and motion

He landed then startled
at the bird bath filled just yesterday
a gift meant for him

I held my breath.
a creak of the door
he flew then perched
on the fence, eyes watching
he swoops in towards the water again
comes and goes in a a skittish pulse
of feather and wing,
though earlier he pounded the trees
here I am, let the world listen

And still, he vanishes
at the whisper of a door
the most common of woodpeckers
spectacular just the same
a flash of beauty eyes following him
back into the woods

Eliza Segiet

Eliza Segiet

Eliza Segiet graduated with a Master's Degree in Philosophy at Jagiellonian University.

Received *Global Literature Guardian Award* – from Motivational Strips, World Nations Writers Union and Union Hispanomundial De Escritores (UHE) 2018.

Nominated for the Pushcart Prize 2019, 2021.

Laureate *Naji Naaman Literary Prize 2020*,

International Award Paragon of Hope (2020),

World Award 2020 *Cesar Vallejo* for Literary Excellence. Laureate of the Special Jury *Sahitto International Award* 2021, World Award *Premiul Fănuș Neagu* 2021.

Finalist *Golden Aster Book* World Literary Prize 2020, *Mili Dueli* 2022, Voci nel deserto 2022.

At the international Festival of Poetry CAMPIONATO MONDIALE DI POESIA (2021/2022) she won the title of vice-champion of the world.

Award BHARAT RATNA RABINDRANATH TAGORE INTERNATIONAL AWARD (2022).

Award - *World Poets Association* (2023).

Laureate Between words and infinity *"International Literary Award (2023).*

Eliza Segiet

The Family Pulse

In the rhythm of life,
there are hardships and moments of peace,
thickets and flowering meadows,
sorrows and joys.

After sleepless nights,
spent by the bed of a sick child,
the time for peace has come.
The starry sky
delights you again.

Before, no one looked up,
the dim light of the nursery
was enough to soften the pulse of the family.

Problems take away the need for the beauty that's around us,
Their absence illuminates even the shadows of the trees,
and awakens the desire to act.

Translated by Dorota Stępińska

Proof

We are not made of clay.
We have a visible body
and a hidden heart –
these are our true attributes.
After all, clothes reveal not much more
than our taste.
To truly show yourself,
you must see Others.

Understanding the Other
and extending a helping hand
is proof
that there is
– Man in a Human Being.

Translated by Dorota Stępińska

Eliza Segiet

The Green of the Grass

Were there words that
could soothe the loss?

Her mirror of reality
was one-dimensional,
always reflecting
absence.
On that June day,
she made a decision.

And…

…she began to see
the green of the grass and the blue of the sky.
The future was born.

The beginning of a full life
– is a smile.

Translated by Dorota Stępińska

William S. Peters Sr.

William S. Peters, Sr.

Bill's writing career spans a period of well over 50 years. Being first Published in 1972, Bill has since went on to Author in excess of 50+ additional Volumes of Poetry, Short Stories, etc., expressing his thoughts on matters of the Heart, Spirit, Consciousness and Humanity. His primary focus is that of Love, Peace and Understanding!

Bill says . . .

I have always likened Life to that of a Garden. So, for me, Life is simply about the Seeds we Sow and Nourish. All things we "Think and Do", will "Be" Cause and eventually manifest itself to being an "Effect" within our own personal "Existences" and "Experiences" . . . whether it be Fruit, Flowers, Weeds or Barren Landscapes! Bill highly regards the Fruits of his Labor and wishes that everyone would thus go on to plant "Lovely" Seeds on "Good Ground" in their own Gardens of Life!

to connect with Bill, he is all things Inner Child

www.iaminnerchild.com

Personal Web Site

www.iamjustbill.com

Bitter - Sweet

In life we have somewhat become aclimated
To accept the Bitter
With the Sweet

Some times
We lie down
And accept the fate
Our existence yeilds unto us ...
At other times
We fight against
What may prove to be
The inevitable

I have found that
When life gives unto me Lemons
To just add a little sugar

Wanted

Like most sentient souls
That express through the flesh,
I wanted,
But I failed to be believe

My desires ruled my kingdom
And like small brush fires
They were easily extinguished

As they say,
The flesh is weak,
And to this
I can attest
To this lower self of mine
That exists it seems
To serve temporal things

The children laugh
The bees pollinate
And collect the nectar
Only to be stolen by
Future realities

Wanted

Such is the purpose
Of Flowers and Butterflies
WrittenInPain

Together

It was not what I expected,
But she allowed me
To have a presence in her life
Anyway

Each day, each night
I am blessed ...
We rise
Together,
We lay ourselves to rest
Together
And all in between
We are
Together

This is the foundation
Of a special type of love.
There is she,
And there is me
And Together
We are one
Together

May 2025 Featured Poets

~ * ~

Swayam Prashant

Ngozi Olivia Osuoha

Kazimierz Burnat

Deepak Kumar Dey

Swayam Prashant

Swayam Prashant

Swayam Prashant (pen name of Dr. Prashanta Kumar Sahoo) was born in the undivided Cuttack district, Odisha. He was formerly an Associate Professor of English, Sarupathar College, Assam, India. He has written ten books including *Heart of Love* (poetry)(published in USA in March 2023); *Premras Amrit* (poetry in Assamese) and *The Sky Conquerors* (2024).

His poems have also been published in several international anthologies like *Being Human* (2024), *Love Letters in Poetic Verse* (2023) and *Light-Bringer* (2024) and in journals like *Impspired* (UK), *Open Skies Quarterly* (USA), *Raven Cage* (Germany) and *The Year of the Poet* (USA).

Email ID : swayam.prashant2001@gmail.com

To Afru With Love

Your lips are red

So is your love

Nay, your love is so red

You need no rose

O O my love,

You are a red red rose !

A Piece of My Heart

I took the snap of an image
reflected in my heart
and put the photograph on display.
All came and praised it profusely.
It must be the photo
of a Queen of an ancient empire,
they said.
I painted a portrait
with the colours of my heart
and put the painting on display.
All came and admired it endlessly.
It must be the painting
of Aphrodite, the Greek goddess of love,
they said.

I took a piece of my heart
and carved a sculpture out of it
and put it on display.
All came and were enchanted with its beauty.
It must be the sculpture
of a divine angel,
they said.

No one said
that it was of you
for no one had ever seen you.
You were always
in my heart
and had never
come out.

The Heart-shaped Rose

You are my heart-shaped rose

you flower in the seeds of silence in solitude

you sing in the pendulum of swinging eternity

you dance in the whirlpool of courting warm waves.

You are my heart-shaped rose

you love, you flirt, you come, you go

but you live in the heart

of my imagination

forever.

Ngozi Olivia Osuoha

Ngozi Olivia Osuoha

Ngozi Olivia Osuoha is a Nigerian poet, writer, thinker, hymnist, and an award winning anthologist. She has authored 28 poetry books, all published outside Nigeria. She has published over 350 poems, articles and essays in over 50 countries. Some of her pieces have been translated in over 16 languages. She has some books in foreign libraries including the US Library of Congress. She is Best Of The Net and Pushcart Nominees. She is a graduate of Estate Management, with some experience in Banking, Broadcasting and tailoring.

Ngozi Olivia Osuoha

Borno Is Not Damned

There is a dam, that needs a ram
It is flooring and fluctuating,
No, Borno is not damned.

It breathes and snores, raging in anger
Flooding aloud, and chasing the crowd,
No, Borno is not damned.

Foot, boots, and hoofs on the roofs,
Daring the days, endangering the genders
No, Borno is not damned.

Land and sea at won with each other
Men and beasts in total commotion,
No, Borno is not damned.

Dam, you can take the ram
And spare men and women,
Dam, you can take the ram
And spare children and property.

Borno is not damned
Dear Borno, you can't be damned
You have had more than enough,
Arise and shine, shine and rise!

Please let Aso rock on you
Rather than Alo flooding you,
Oh Borno, let your shine shine again.

Borno The Home Of Peace

Borno will not be damned
These raging waters shall settle,
And your land shall know peace again.

Borno, the land of peace
Ahoy! How alloys destroy,
Bullets shall never again rock
For peace is now come!

Borno, these waters shall still,
No more shall dams distress you
Floodgates of heaven shall water your seed.

Borno, look at the rainbow
The shine is here
The day has come
Oh, the dawn is risen.

Borno, the land of peace
You shall not sink
Lift up your gates,
And let this newness emerge!

This sweeping shall be, never again
Receive pureness and brightness
Borno, enough is your pain
Peace, be still
Calm for calamity.

Ngozi Olivia Osuoha

Dear Dele Farotimi

To class, eloquence, and intelligence I write.
To truthfulness, clarity, and talent, still I write.
To wisdom, knowledge, and versatility I also write.
To a great gift, I humbly write,
It is indeed an honour to write you.

The sincerity in your mission
And the clarity of your facts,
The weight on your passion
And the volume of the quest;
I write to honour your rarity.

The maturity in your vision
And the uniqueness of your voice,
What an honour to write this!

Above tribal sentiments and religious bias
Despite cultural boundaries and occupational hazards
Beyond selfish interests and personal goals;
Oh how blessed the womb that bore you!

I love how hard your words are; concrete
I like how black you are; unwashable.
I celebrate the man you are; legend.
I appreciate the Africa in you, hero.
What an honour to write you!

Kazimierz Burnat

Kazimierz Burnat

Kazimierz Burnat is a prominent poet, essayist, translator, journalist, literary critic, and culture animator born in Szczepanowice on the Dunajec River. From 2015, president of the Lower Silesian Branch of ZLP (Polish Writers' Union) in Wrocław. Creator of scouting for difficult youth as part of *The Untrodden Trail*. Guardian of Places of National Remembrance; his life mottos are: remembering the dead—the source of longevity; doing good—the path to humanity.

Author of 23 books of poetry, including 7 translations from Czech and Ukrainian, and over 60 collective books with translations of works from these languages, as well as Belarusian, Russian, Slovenian and Hungarian. He edited and provided an afterword or introduction to over 90 different books. Co-author of approximately 370 anthologies and monographs. Translated into over 43 foreign languages. Instructor of literary workshops, juror of competitions. Organizer or co-organizer and active participant of numerous national and international festivals and literary meetings. For years, organizer of the International Poetry Festival "Poets Without Borders" in Polanica Zdrój. Initiator and organizer of cultural cooperation with the National Union of Writers of Ukraine. He received several Ukrainian Literary Awards for translation activity and popularization of Ukrainian literature abroad, as well as for his own literary output and significant contribution to the revival of spirituality and culture of the Ukrainian nation. […]

Kazimierz Burnat

Retreat

I am afraid of lost time
it intensifies the malaise
of an escape into creativity
and one needs to immerse oneself in it
compulsively desperately
to enslave fear
out of books building a barricade
against the massacred truth
against hatred

writing – a nightmare
I have become a poet
requiring correction
and changes
pinch authenticity

I must necessarily
engraft wild words
overheard in dreams
to anew be able to
express myself and the world
in the best possible way

Translated by Anna Maria Stępień

Not death separates people, but lack of love. ~ Jim Morrison

Love
is wild flowers
simplicity-colored

the sky's clear azure

soul and flesh entwined
by a flimsy unity

it is you and him
in the glow of trust
showing the common path
to Sesame

love
is an ebony tunnel
with bedazzlement at the end

not seeing
will arouse new sensations

Translated by Anna Maria Stępień

Kazimierz Burnat

Wrongheadedness

Discouraged by waiting
for prosperity
they abandon the pretense of bonds

though unripe are the common fruit
ready to pollinate
wayside flowers
already burdened with a flaw

distrust
makes them the carriers of hatred
indwelling the innermost resources

and so
nestled into foreign tenderness
hearing the pulse bubbling
of leaky hearts
they savor the image of unfulfillment

from breathlessness
souls grow blue

the final wake-up call
for a compromise lesson

Translated by Anna Maria Stępień

Deepak Kumar Dey

Deepak Kumar Dey

Deepak Kumar Dey, son of late Dr. G. C. Dey and Late Surama Dey, hails from Bagdia, Angul district of Odisha, is an ardent lover of nature and avid worshipper of poetry He was a student of chemical engineering but passion of poetry attracted him to search divine bliss in nature. Since he has crossed many ordeals in his life and hazardous brusqueness yet he finds supreme God's benevolent presence and prudence. He never looks for social status or recognition. Through soulfulness he seeks Almighty's abundant grace and mercies. In arrayed words he weaves the magic of mirthful munificence and glory of God. He gives in before the God to be in His pupillage. His poems have been published in 65 national and international anthologies and many UGC approved journals; in both Odia and English.

Solemn Proclamation

Solemn I am, privately wish -
    To be a gardener
    To enthrone some flowers to bloom-
    Of consciousness;
    Omni direction will be exhilarating
    By its fragrant beautifulness;
    Individuality shall stand over-
    Summed love and abundant fearlessness.

Solemn I am and do aspire-
    To be a sculptor
    And to do up a fine architecture-
    By an artistic calligraph,
    Which will have no line on vast
    Canvas,
    Connected with edgeless
    Geographic perimeter;
    After all, there will be - be all
    And end all; compassionate stall,
    Few and far between cultural call.

Solemn I am, for cause of purity
    I wish to be a poet-
    To write in black and white
    Such a poem of which-
    Every word will utter for liberty;
    And by speaketh utterance
    Will be vanquished all ill substances
    From human beings' mind,
    And the whole universe will be-
    Blended in season and out of season.

History

History is sleeping in deep slumber
Being tired after prevailing undone
As if no work is left to be done in future.

In frantically toxicated blood of earth
Everything is dead or tired
That was supposed to be transmitted
As if there is no death further.

Slunk off history is lying down straight like dead,
A green field is tangled into womb of sky,
Which is not visible farther;
Softened and heart-rending life
Is wrapped up by slightest snowy feather.
Neither light nor darkness is found,
Stranded and silent greenish field
And only there is ocular capital and shield
Of screaming history.

In deep sleep is history
As if there is no absurd work,
Devilish massacre or clattering from soldiers,
Unlawful mockery and unmannerly behaviour
Or booming from hunger eater and scorching fear
Or shrilling voice in crackling condolences
Nothing will be happened,
Neither unholy exploitation nor extortionists presence.

So innocent than a dead man
The physique of history,
And limitless wide open vast green land
Dilated in outdated dreamless hand
Upon evergreen breast of darkened sand.

Gambling ogre and demons have returned back to history,
Not a single dust particle will be seen in oblation at death of history.

Have they reached at home!!

Only this message:
'They had set out ',
Have they reached at home?
This python like road is outstretched
Unendingly, No one is at sight.

Still,
Unlike vibrating rails sound,
If ears are put on curvy ground,
Rush in rash so fast who could?

Had their feet been dissolved on way?
Is not this vibration of a heart -
Approaching to comely childhood,
A butterfly - cliche to a statue?

This's heard about ongoing battle
But no news when it will come to an end.
Shaken hands looking inwards with lifeless,
Wedded promise turns to wind up warfare song,
Assurance that's turned Gandhari will be sung;
Slowly if they're lifeless, for whom and why;
Who is friend and who is enemy,
Where cantonment is unseen to eye.

They had waved upon to deal with,
On barefoot, bullock cart to battle ground
To reveal violent take
Arrow filled quiver and bow
Armour of readiness to make
To triumph over heads;
To win was different,
On strange canvas feet did melt.

Deepak Kumar Dey

All feet have not returned back
Some slided along mirage
Becoming poem and epitaph's
Last stanza.
If anyone finds their synopsis
Let it know to any poet;
May he compose gist and sing a ghazal
During mid-day or lonely night.

Remembering

our fallen soldiers of verse

Janet Perkins Caldwell
February 14, 1959 ~ September 20, 2016

Alan W. Jankowski
16 March 1961 ~ 10 March 2017

Shareef Abdur Rasheed
30 May 1945 ~ 11 February 2025

The Butterfly Effect

"IS" in effect

Inner Child Press

News

Published Books

by

Poetry Posse Members

We are so excited to share and announce a few of the current books, as well as the new and upcoming books of some of our Poetry Posse authors.

Inner Child Press News

On the following pages we present to you ...

Alicja Maria Kuberska

Jackie Davis Allen

Gail Weston Shazor

hülya n. yılmaz

Nizar Sartawi

Elizabeth E. Castillo

Faleeha Hassan

Fahredin Shehu

Kimberly Burnham

Caroline 'Ceri' Nazareno

Eliza Segiet

Teresa E. Gallion

Mutawaf Shaheed

William S. Peters, Sr.

Now Available
www.innerchildpress.com

The Year of the Poet XII ~ May 2025

KREW ŻYCIA

The Blood of Life

Eliza Segiet

Translated by Dorota Stępińska

Now Available
www.innerchildpress.com

Inner Child Press News

Now Available
www.innerchildpress.com

The Year of the Poet XII ~ May 2025

Now Available
www.innerchildpress.com

Inner Child Press News

Now Available
www.innerchildpress.com

The Year of the Poet XII ~ May 2025

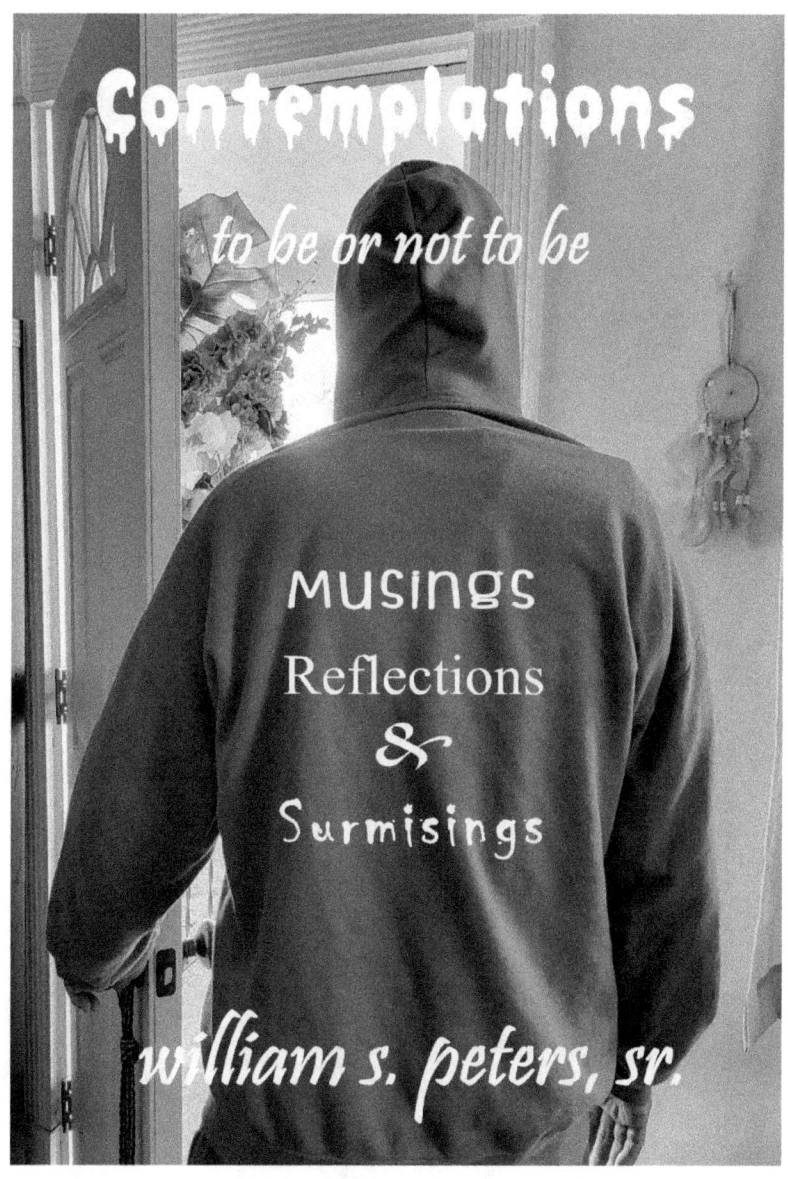

Now Available
www.innerchildpress.com

Inner Child Press News

Now Available
www.innerchildpress.com

The Year of the Poet XII ~ May 2025

Now Available
www.innerchildpress.com

Inner Child Press News

Now Available
www.innerchildpress.com

The Year of the Poet XII ~ May 2025

Now Available
www.innerchildpress.com

Inner Child Press News

Now Available
www.innerchildpress.com

The Year of the Poet XII ~ May 2025

Now Available
www.innerchildpress.com

Inner Child Press News

Now Available
www.innerchildpress.com

The Year of the Poet XII ~ May 2025

Now Available
www.innerchildpress.com

Inner Child Press News

Now Available at
www.innerchildpress.com

The Year of the Poet XII ~ May 2025

Now Available at

www.amazon.com/gp/product/B08MYL5B7S/ref=dbs_a_def_rwt_hsch_vapi_tkin_p1_i2

Inner Child Press News

Now Available
www.innerchildpress.com

The Year of the Poet XII ~ May 2025

Now Available
www.innerchildpress.com

Inner Child Press News

Now Available
www.innerchildpress.com

The Year of the Poet XII ~ May 2025

Now Available
www.innerchildpress.com

Inner Child Press News

Now Available
www.innerchildpress.com

The Year of the Poet XII ~ May 2025

Now Available
www.innerchildpress.com

Inner Child Press News

Now Available
www.innerchildpress.com

The Year of the Poet XII ~ May 2025

Now Available
www.innerchildpress.com

Inner Child Press News

Now Available
www.innerchildpress.com

The Year of the Poet XII ~ May 2025

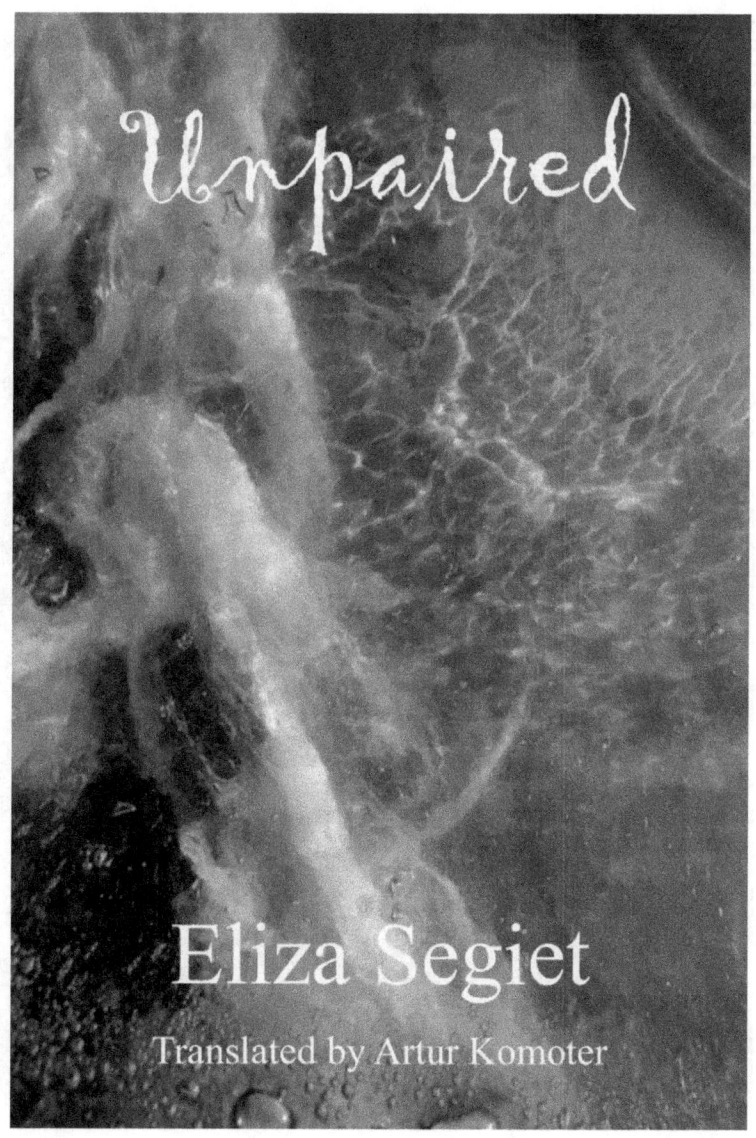

Now Available
www.innerchildpress.com

Inner Child Press News

Private Issue
www.innerchildpress.com

The Year of the Poet XII ~ May 2025

Now Available at
www.innerchildpress.com

Inner Child Press News

No Illusions
Through the Looking Glass

Jackie Davis Allen

Now Available at
www.innerchildpress.com

The Year of the Poet XII ~ May 2025

Now Available at
www.innerchildpress.com

Inner Child Press News

Now Available at
www.innerchildpress.com

The Year of the Poet XII ~ May 2025

HERENOW

FAHREDIN SHEHU

Now Available at
www.innerchildpress.com

Inner Child Press News

Now Available at
www.innerchildpress.com

The Year of the Poet XII ~ May 2025

Now Available at
www.innerchildpress.com

Inner Child Press News

Now Available at
www.innerchildpress.com

The Year of the Poet XII ~ May 2025

Now Available at
www.innerchildpress.com

Inner Child Press News

Now Available at
www.innerchildpress.com

The Year of the Poet XII ~ May 2025

Now Available at
www.innerchildpress.com

Inner Child Press News

Now Available at
www.innerchildpress.com

The Year of the Poet XII ~ May 2025

Now Available at
www.innerchildpress.com

Inner Child Press News

Now Available at
www.innerchildpress.com

The Year of the Poet XII ~ May 2025

Now Available at
www.innerchildpress.com

Inner Child Press News

Now Available
www.innerchildpress.com

Other Anthological works from

Inner Child Press International

www.innerchildpress.com

Inner Child Press Anthologies

Shareef
a soldier for
Allah

Patriarch, Activist & Humanitarian

Friends of the Pen

Now Available
www.innerchildpress.com/anthologies

Inner Child Press Anthologies

Now Available
www.innerchildpress.com

Inner Child Press Anthologies

Now Available
www.innerchildpress.com/anthologies

Inner Child Press Anthologies

Now Available
www.innerchildpress.com/anthologies

Inner Child Press Anthologies

Now Available
www.worldhealingworldpeacepoetry.com

Inner Child Press Anthologies

Now Available
www.innerchildpress.com/anthologies

Inner Child Press Anthologies

Now Available
www.worldhealingworldpeacepoetry.com

Inner Child Press Anthologies

Now Available
www.innerchildpress.com/anthologies

Inner Child Press Anthologies

Inner Child Press International
&
The Year of the Poet
present

Poetry
the best of 2020

Poets of the World

Now Available
www.innerchildpress.com/anthologies

Inner Child Press Anthologies

Now Available
www.innerchildpress.com/anthologies

Inner Child Press Anthologies

Now Available
www.innerchildpress.com/anthologies

Inner Child Press Anthologies

Now Available
www.innerchildpress.com/anthologies

Inner Child Press Anthologies

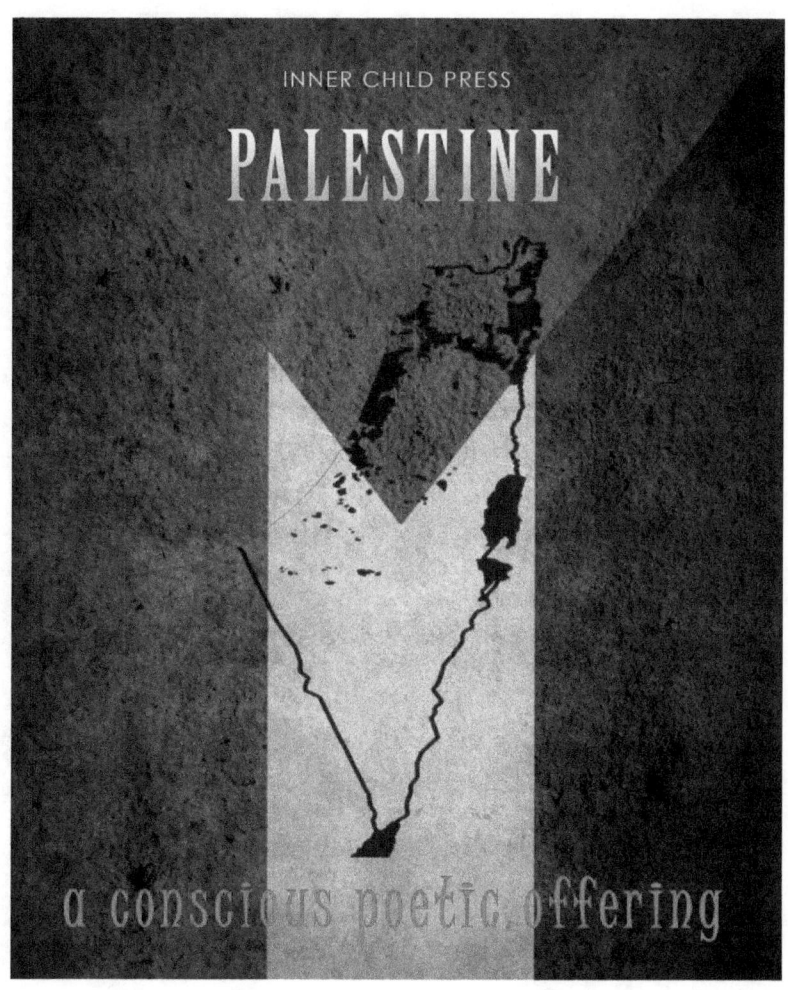

Now Available
www.innerchildpress.com/anthologies

Inner Child Press Anthologies

Now Available
www.innerchildpress.com/anthologies

Inner Child Press Anthologies

Now Available
www.innerchildpress.com/anthologies

Inner Child Press Anthologies

Now Available
www.worldhealingworldpeacepoetry.com

Inner Child Press Anthologies

Now Available

www.worldhealingworldpeacepoetry.com

Inner Child Press Anthologies

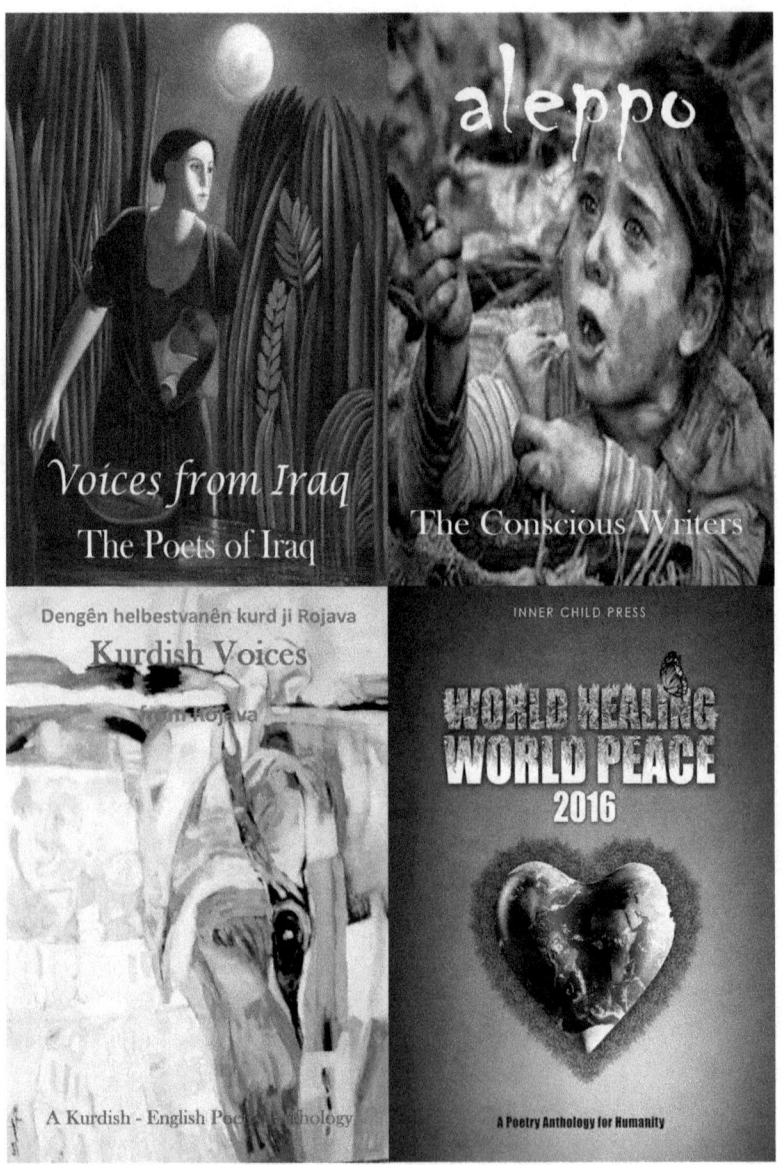

Now Available
www.innerchildpress.com/anthologies

Inner Child Press Anthologies

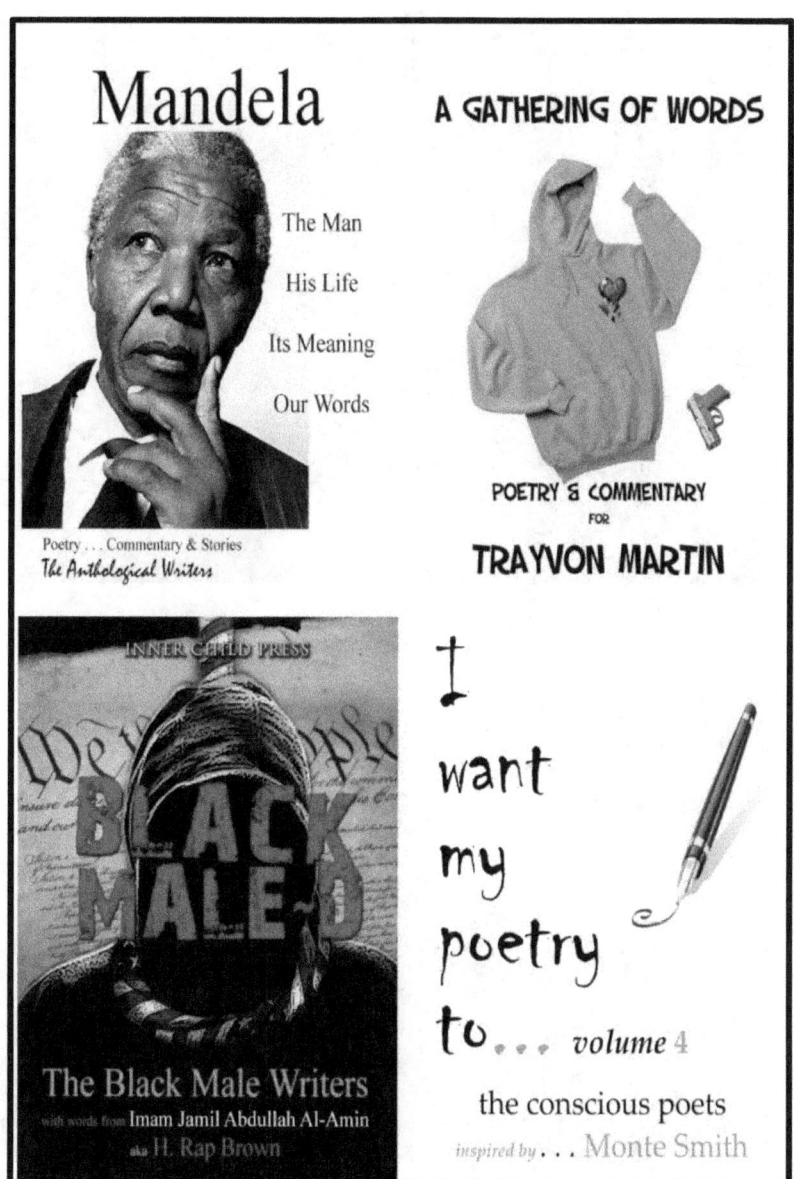

Now Available
www.innerchildpress.com/anthologies

Inner Child Press Anthologies

Now Available
www.innerchildpress.com/anthologies

Inner Child Press Anthologies

Now Available
www.innerchildpress.com/anthologies

Inner Child Press Anthologies

Now Available
www.innerchildpress.com/anthologies

Inner Child Press Anthologies

Now Available
www.innerchildpress.com/the-year-of-the-poet

Inner Child Press Anthologies

Now Available

www.innerchildpress.com/the-year-of-the-poet

Inner Child Press Anthologies

Now Available
www.innerchildpress.com/the-year-of-the-poet

Inner Child Press Anthologies

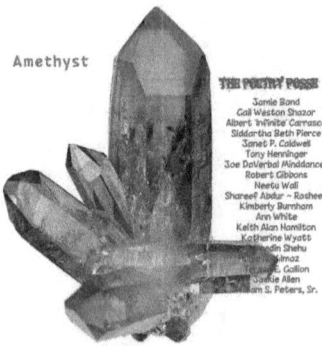

Now Available

www.innerchildpress.com/the-year-of-the-poet

Inner Child Press Anthologies

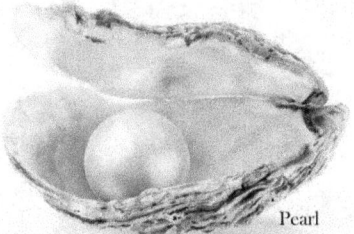

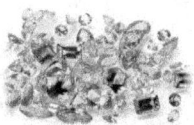

Now Available
www.innerchildpress.com/the-year-of-the-poet

Inner Child Press Anthologies

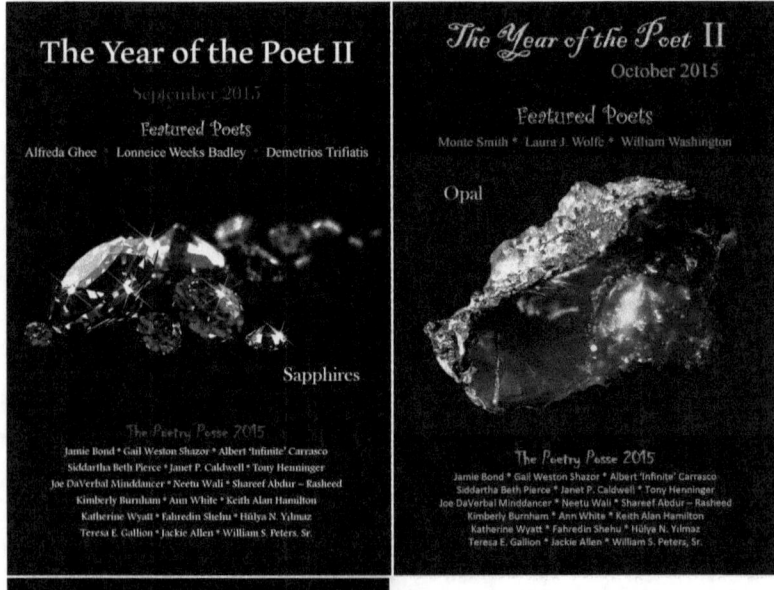

Now Available
www.innerchildpress.com/the-year-of-the-poet

Inner Child Press Anthologies

Now Available
www.innerchildpress.com/the-year-of-the-poet

Inner Child Press Anthologies

Now Available
www.innerchildpress.com/the-year-of-the-poet

Inner Child Press Anthologies

Now Available
www.innerchildpress.com/the-year-of-the-poet

Inner Child Press Anthologies

Now Available
www.innerchildpress.com/the-year-of-the-poet

Inner Child Press Anthologies

Now Available
www.innerchildpress.com/the-year-of-the-poet

Inner Child Press Anthologies

The Year of the Poet IV
September 2017

Featured Poets
Martina Reisz Newberry
Ameer Nassir
Christine Fulco Neal
Robert Neal

The Elm Tree

The Poetry Posse 2017

Gail Weston Shazor * Caroline Nazareno * Bismay Mohanty
Teresa E. Gallion * Anna Jakubczak Vel Ratty Adalan
Joe DaVerbal Minddancer * Shareef Abdur – Rasheed
Albert Carrasco * Kimberly Burnham * Elizabeth Castillo
Hülya N. Yılmaz * Faleeha Hassan * Jackie Davis Allen
Jen Walls * Nizar Sartawi * * William S. Peters, Sr.

The Year of the Poet IV
October 2017

Featured Poets
Ahmed Abu Saleem
Nedal Al-Qaeim
Sadeddin Shahin

The Black Walnut Tree

The Poetry Posse 2017

Gail Weston Shazor * Caroline Nazareno * Bismay Mohanty
Teresa E. Gallion * Anna Jakubczak Vel Ratty Adalan
Joe DaVerbal Minddancer * Shareef Abdur – Rasheed
Albert Carrasco * Kimberly Burnham * Elizabeth Castillo
Hülya N. Yılmaz * Faleeha Hassan * Jackie Davis Allen
Jen Walls * Nizar Sartawi * William S. Peters, Sr.

The Year of the Poet IV
November 2017

Featured Poets
Kay Peters
Alfreda D. Ghee
Gabriella Garofalo
Rosemary Cappello

The Tree of Life

The Poetry Posse 2017

Gail Weston Shazor * Caroline Nazareno * Bismay Mohanty
Teresa E. Gallion * Anna Jakubczak Vel Ratty Adalan
Joe DaVerbal Minddancer * Shareef Abdur – Rasheed
Albert Carrasco * Kimberly Burnham * Elizabeth Castillo
Hülya N. Yılmaz * Faleeha Hassan * Jackie Davis Allen
Jen Walls * Nizar Sartawi * William S. Peters, Sr.

The Year of the Poet IV
December 2017

Featured Poets
Justice Clarke
Mariel M. Pabroa
Kiley Brown

The Fig Tree

The Poetry Posse 2017

Gail Weston Shazor * Caroline Nazareno * Bismay Mohanty
Teresa E. Gallion * Anna Jakubczak Vel Ratty Adalan
Joe DaVerbal Minddancer * Shareef Abdur – Rasheed
Albert Carrasco * Kimberly Burnham * Elizabeth Castillo
Hülya N. Yılmaz * Faleeha Hassan * Jackie Davis Allen
Jen Walls * Nizar Sartawi * William S. Peters, Sr.

Now Available

www.innerchildpress.com/the-year-of-the-poet

Inner Child Press Anthologies

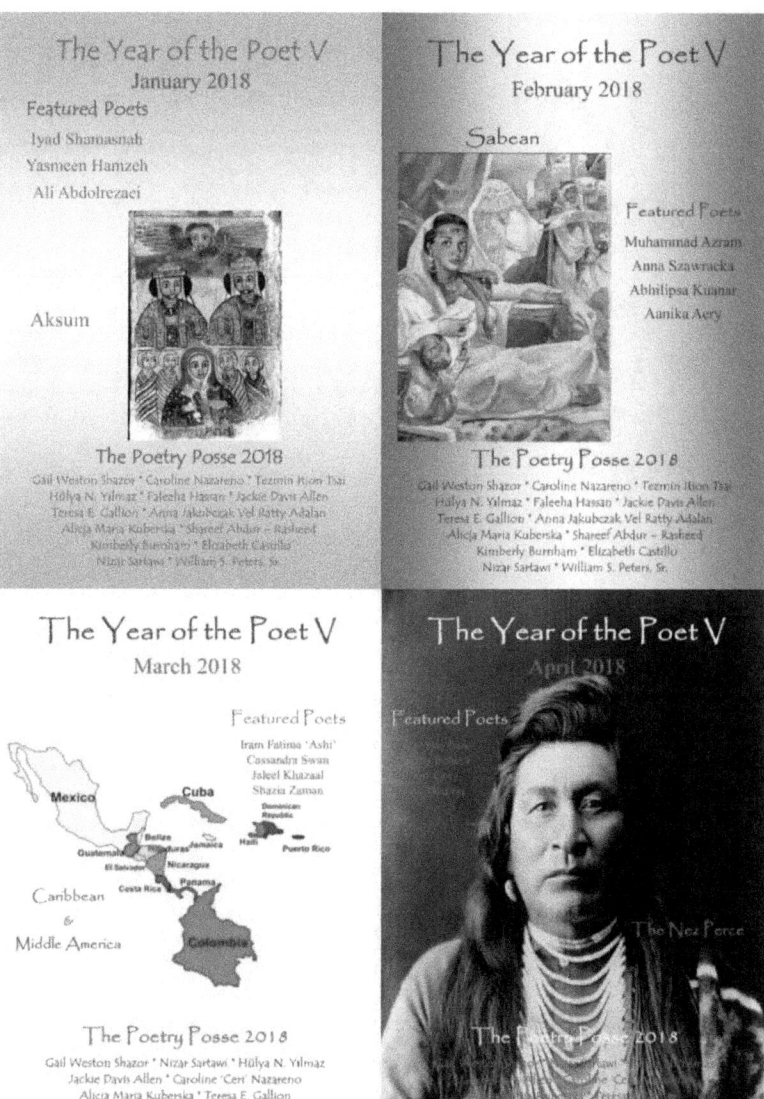

Now Available

www.innerchildpress.com/the-year-of-the-poet

Inner Child Press Anthologies

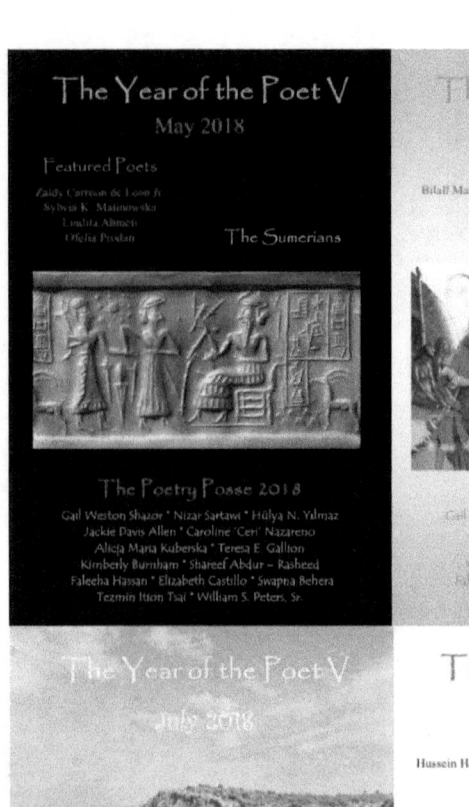

Now Available

www.innerchildpress.com/the-year-of-the-poet

Inner Child Press Anthologies

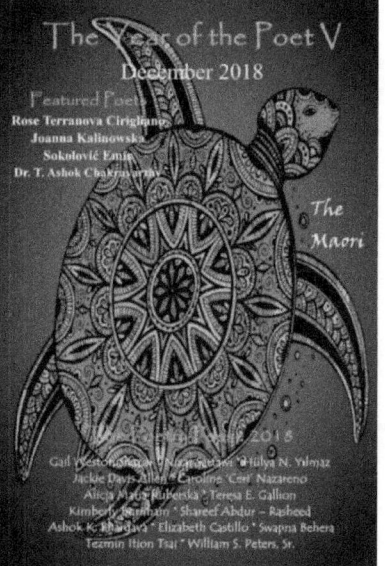

Now Available
www.innerchildpress.com/the-year-of-the-poet

Inner Child Press Anthologies

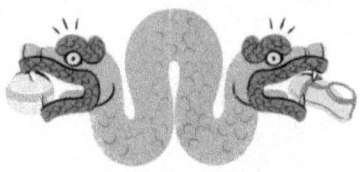
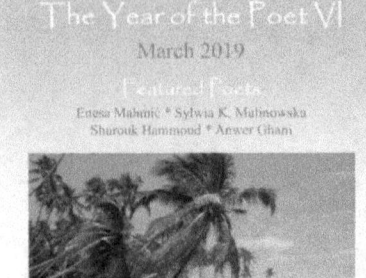
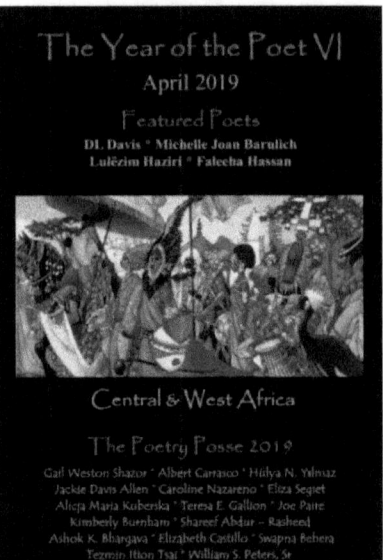

Now Available

www.innerchildpress.com/the-year-of-the-poet

Inner Child Press Anthologies

Now Available
www.innerchildpress.com/the-year-of-the-poet

Inner Child Press Anthologies

Now Available
www.innerchildpress.com/the-year-of-the-poet

Inner Child Press Anthologies

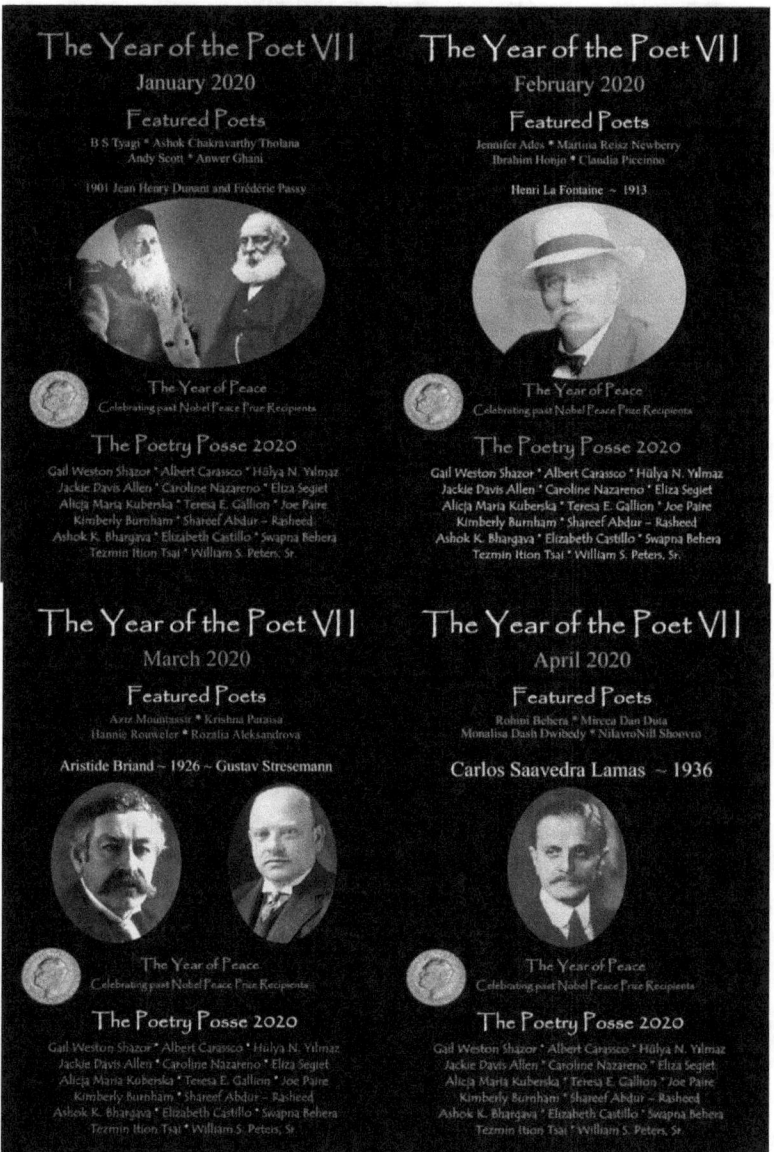

Now Available
www.innerchildpress.com/the-year-of-the-poet

Inner Child Press Anthologies

The Year of the Poet VII
May 2020

Featured Poets
Alok Kumar Ray * Eden S. Trinidad
Franco Barbato * Izabela Zubko

Ralph Bunche ~ 1950

The Year of Peace
Celebrating past Nobel Peace Prize Recipients

The Poetry Posse 2020
Gail Weston Shazor * Albert Carasco * Hülya N. Yılmaz
Jackie Davis Allen * Caroline Nazareno * Eliza Segiet
Alicja Maria Kuberska * Teresa E. Gallion * Joe Paire
Kimberly Burnham * Shareef Abdur – Rasheed
Ashok K. Bhargava * Elizabeth Castillo * Swapna Behera
Tezmin Ition Tsai * William S. Peters, Sr.

The Year of the Poet VII
June 2020

Featured Poets
Eftichia Kapardeli * Metin Cengiz
Hussein Habasch * Kosh K Mathew

Albert John Lutuli ~ 1960

The Year of Peace
Celebrating past Nobel Peace Prize Recipients

The Poetry Posse 2020
Gail Weston Shazor * Albert Carasco * Hülya N. Yılmaz
Jackie Davis Allen * Caroline Nazareno * Eliza Segiet
Alicja Maria Kuberska * Teresa E. Gallion * Joe Paire
Kimberly Burnham * Shareef Abdur – Rasheed
Ashok K. Bhargava * Elizabeth Castillo * Swapna Behera
Tezmin Ition Tsai * William S. Peters, Sr.

The Year of the Poet VII
July 2020

Featured Poets
Mykola Martyniuk * Orbindu Ganga
Roula Pollard * Karn Praktisha

Norman Ernest Borlaug ~ 1970

The Year of Peace
Celebrating past Nobel Peace Prize Recipients

The Poetry Posse 2020
Gail Weston Shazor * Albert Carasco * Hülya N. Yılmaz
Jackie Davis Allen * Caroline Nazareno * Eliza Segiet
Alicja Maria Kuberska * Teresa E. Gallion * Joe Paire
Kimberly Burnham * Shareef Abdur – Rasheed
Ashok K. Bhargava * Elizabeth Castillo * Swapna Behera
Tezmin Ition Tsai * William S. Peters, Sr.

The Year of the Poet VII
August 2020

Featured Poets
Dr Pragya Suman * Chinh Nguyen
Srinivas Vasudev * Ugwu Leonard Ifeanyi, Jr.

Adolfo Pérez Esquivel ~ 1980

The Year of Peace
Celebrating past Nobel Peace Prize Recipients

The Poetry Posse 2020
Gail Weston Shazor * Albert Carasco * Hülya N. Yılmaz
Jackie Davis Allen * Caroline Nazareno * Eliza Segiet
Alicja Maria Kuberska * Teresa E. Gallion * Joe Paire
Kimberly Burnham * Shareef Abdur – Rasheed
Ashok K. Bhargava * Elizabeth Castillo * Swapna Behera
Tezmin Ition Tsai * William S. Peters, Sr.

Now Available
www.innerchildpress.com/the-year-of-the-poet

Inner Child Press Anthologies

Now Available
www.innerchildpress.com/the-year-of-the-poet

Inner Child Press Anthologies

Now Available
www.innerchildpress.com/the-year-of-the-poet

Inner Child Press Anthologies

The Year of the Poet VIII
May 2021

Featured Global Poets
Paramita Mukherjee Mullick * Rose Zerguine
Jaydeep Sarangi * Bismay Mohanty

Diego Rivera

Poetry ... Ekphrasticly Speaking

The Poetry Posse 2021

Gail Weston Shazor * Albert Carasco * Hülya N. Yılmaz
Jackie Davis Allen * Caroline Nazareno * Eliza Segiet
Alicja Maria Kuberska * Teresa E. Gallion * Joe Paire
Kimberly Burnham * Shareef Abdur – Rasheed
Ashok K. Bhargava * Elizabeth Castillo * Swapna Behera
Tezmin Ition Tsai * William S. Peters, Sr.

The Year of the Poet VIII
June 2021

Featured Global Poets
Alonzo "zO" Gross * Lali Tsipi Michaeli
Tareq al Karmy * Tirthendu Ganguly

Rayen Kang

 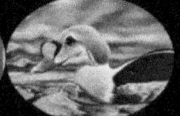

Poetry ... Ekphrasticly Speaking

The Poetry Posse 2021

Gail Weston Shazor * Albert Carasco * Hülya N. Yılmaz
Jackie Davis Allen * Caroline Nazareno * Eliza Segiet
Alicja Maria Kuberska * Teresa E. Gallion * Joe Paire
Kimberly Burnham * Shareef Abdur – Rasheed
Ashok K. Bhargava * Elizabeth Castillo * Swapna Behera
Tezmin Ition Tsai * William S. Peters, Sr.

The Year of the Poet VIII
July 2021

Featured Global Poets
Iram Jaan * Vesna Mundishevska-Veljanovska
Ngozi Olivia Osuoha * Lan Qyqalla

Goncalao Mabunda

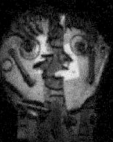

Poetry ... Ekphrasticly Speaking

The Poetry Posse 2021

Gail Weston Shazor * Albert Carasco * Hülya N. Yılmaz
Jackie Davis Allen * Caroline Nazareno * Eliza Segiet
Alicja Maria Kuberska * Teresa E. Gallion * Joe Paire
Kimberly Burnham * Shareef Abdur – Rasheed
Ashok K. Bhargava * Elizabeth Castillo * Swapna Behera
Tezmin Ition Tsai * William S. Peters, Sr.

The Year of the Poet VIII
August 2021

Featured Global Poets
Caroline Laurent Turunc * Kamal Dhungana
Pankhuri Sinha * Paramita Mukherjee Mullick

Mundara Koorang

Poetry ... Ekphrasticly Speaking

The Poetry Posse 2021

Gail Weston Shazor * Albert Carasco * Hülya N. Yılmaz
Jackie Davis Allen * Caroline Nazareno * Eliza Segiet
Alicja Maria Kuberska * Teresa E. Gallion * Joe Paire
Kimberly Burnham * Shareef Abdur – Rasheed
Ashok K. Bhargava * Elizabeth Castillo * Swapna Behera
Tezmin Ition Tsai * William S. Peters, Sr.

Now Available

www.innerchildpress.com/the-year-of-the-poet

Inner Child Press Anthologies

Now Available

www.innerchildpress.com/the-year-of-the-poet

Inner Child Press Anthologies

The Year of the Poet IX
January 2022

Featured Global Poets
**Ratan Ghosh * Christine Neil-Wright
Andrew Scott * Ashok Kumar**

Climate Change : The Ice Cap

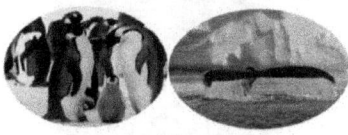

Poetry . . . Ekphrasticly Speaking

The Poetry Posse 2021

Gail Weston Shazor * Albert Carasco * Hülya N. Yılmaz
Jackie Davis Allen * Caroline Nazareno * Eliza Segiet
Alicja Maria Kuberska * Teresa E. Gallion * Joe Paire
Kimberly Burnham * Shareef Abdur – Rasheed
Ashok K. Bhargava * Elizabeth Castillo * Swapna Behera
Tezmin Ition Tsai * William S. Peters, Sr.

The Year of the Poet IX
February 2022

Featured Global Poets
Roza Boyanova *·Ramón de Jesús Núñez Duval
Mammad Ismayil * Tarana Turan Rahimli

Climate Change and Mountains

Poetry . . . Ekphrasticly Speaking

The Poetry Posse 2021

Gail Weston Shazor * Albert Carasco * Hülya N. Yılmaz
Jackie Davis Allen * Caroline Nazareno * Eliza Segiet
Alicja Maria Kuberska * Teresa E. Gallion * Joe Paire
Kimberly Burnham * Shareef Abdur – Rasheed
Ashok K. Bhargava * Elizabeth Castillo * Swapna Behera
Tezmin Ition Tsai * William S. Peters, Sr.

The Year of the Poet IX
March 2022

Featured Global Poets
Dimitris P. Kraniotis * Marlene Pasini
Kennedy Ochieng * Swayam Prashant

Climate Change and Space Debris

Poetry . . . Ekphrasticly Speaking

The Poetry Posse 2021

Gail Weston Shazor * Albert Carasco * Hülya N. Yılmaz
Jackie Davis Allen * Caroline Nazareno * Eliza Segiet
Alicja Maria Kuberska * Teresa E. Gallion * Joe Paire
Kimberly Burnham * Shareef Abdur – Rasheed
Ashok K. Bhargava * Elizabeth Castillo * Swapna Behera
Tezmin Ition Tsai * William S. Peters, Sr.

The Year of the Poet IX
April 2022

Featured Global Poets
**Alonzo Gross * Dr. Debaprasanna Biswas
Monsif Beroual * Carol Aronoff**

Climate Change and Oceans

Celebrating our 100th Edition

Poetry . . . Ekphrasticly Speaking

The Poetry Posse 2021

Gail Weston Shazor * Albert Carasco * Hülya N. Yılmaz
Jackie Davis Allen * Caroline Nazareno * Eliza Segiet
Alicja Maria Kuberska * Teresa E. Gallion * Joe Paire
Kimberly Burnham * Shareef Abdur – Rasheed
Ashok K. Bhargava * Elizabeth Castillo * Swapna Behera
Tezmin Ition Tsai * William S. Peters, Sr

Now Available
www.innerchildpress.com/the-year-of-the-poet

Inner Child Press Anthologies

The Year of the Poet IX
May 2022

Featured Global Poets
Ndaba Sibanda * Smrutiranjan Mohanty
Ajanta Paul * Monalisa Dash Dwibedy

Climate Change and Birds

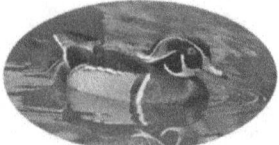

Poetry . . . Ekphrasticly Speaking

The Poetry Posse 2021

Gail Weston Shazor * Albert Carasco * Hülya N. Yılmaz
Jackie Davis Allen * Caroline Nazareno * Eliza Segiet
Alicja Maria Kuberska * Teresa E. Gallion * Joe Paire
Kimberly Burnham * Shareef Abdur – Rasheed
Ashok K. Bhargava * Elizabeth Castillo * Swapna Behera
Tezmin Ition Tsai * William S. Peters, Sr.

The Year of the Poet IX
June 2022

Featured Global Poets
Yuan Changming * Azeezat Okunlola
Tanja Ajtić * Philip Chijioke Abonyi

Climate Change and Trees

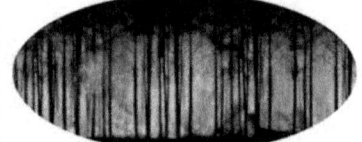

Poetry . . . Ekphrasticly Speaking

The Poetry Posse 2022

Gail Weston Shazor * Albert Carasco * Hülya N. Yılmaz
Jackie Davis Allen * Caroline Nazareno * Eliza Segiet
Alicja Maria Kuberska * Teresa E. Gallion * Joe Paire
Kimberly Burnham * Shareef Abdur – Rasheed
Ashok K. Bhargava * Elizabeth Castillo * Swapna Behera
Tezmin Ition Tsai * William S. Peters, Sr.

The Year of the Poet IX
July 2022

Featured Global Poets
Michelle Joan Barulich * Mili Das
Anna Ferriero * Ujjal Mandal

Climate Change and Animals

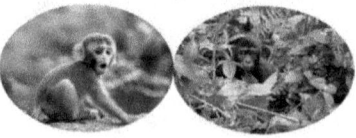

Poetry . . . Ekphrasticly Speaking

The Poetry Posse 2022

Gail Weston Shazor * Albert Carasco * Hülya N. Yılmaz
Jackie Davis Allen * Caroline Nazareno * Eliza Segiet
Alicja Maria Kuberska * Teresa E. Gallion * Joe Paire
Kimberly Burnham * Shareef Abdur – Rasheed
Ashok K. Bhargava * Elizabeth Castillo * Swapna Behera
Tezmin Ition Tsai * William S. Peters, Sr.

The Year of the Poet IX
August 2022

Featured Global Poets
Pankhuri Sinha * Abdulloh Abdumominov
Caroline Turunç * Tali Cohen Shabtai

Climate Change and Agriculture

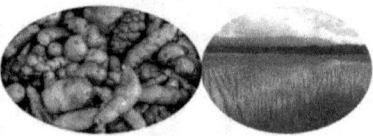

Poetry . . . Ekphrasticly Speaking

The Poetry Posse 2022

Gail Weston Shazor * Albert Carasco * Hülya N. Yılmaz
Jackie Davis Allen * Caroline Nazareno * Eliza Segiet
Alicja Maria Kuberska * Teresa E. Gallion * Joe Paire
Kimberly Burnham * Shareef Abdur – Rasheed
Ashok K. Bhargava * Elizabeth Castillo * Swapna Behera
Tezmin Ition Tsai * William S. Peters, Sr.

Now Available
www.innerchildpress.com/the-year-of-the-poet

Inner Child Press Anthologies

The Year of the Poet IX
September 2022

Featured Global Poets
Ngozi Olivia Osuoha * Biswajit Mishra
Sylwia K. Malinowska * Sajid Hussein

Climate Change and Wind and Weather Patterns

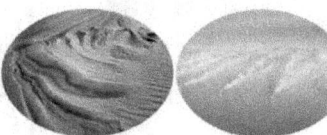

Poetry . . . Ekphrasticly Speaking

The Poetry Posse 2022

Gail Weston Shazor * Albert Carasico * Hülya N. Yılmaz
Jackie Davis Allen * Caroline Nazareno * Eliza Segiet
Alicja Maria Kuberska * Teresa E. Gallion * Joe Paire
Kimberly Burnham * Shareef Abdur – Rasheed
Ashok K. Bhargava * Elizabeth Castillo * Swapna Behera
Tezmin Ition Tsai * William S. Peters, Sr.

The Year of the Poet IX
October 2022

Featured Global Poets
Andrew Kouroupos * Brenda Mohammed
Carthornia Kouroupos * Faleeha Hassan

Climate Change and Oil and Power

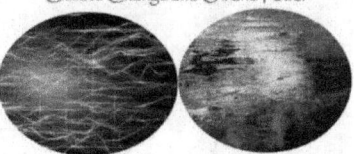

Poetry . . . Ekphrasticly Speaking

The Poetry Posse 2022

Gail Weston Shazor * Albert Carasico * Hülya N. Yılmaz
Jackie Davis Allen * Caroline Nazareno * Eliza Segiet
Alicja Maria Kuberska * Teresa E. Gallion * Joe Paire
Kimberly Burnham * Shareef Abdur – Rasheed
Ashok K. Bhargava * Elizabeth Castillo * Swapna Behera
Tezmin Ition Tsai * William S. Peters, Sr.

The Year of the Poet IX
November 2022

Featured Global Poets
Hema Ravi * Shafkat Aziz Hajam
Selma Kopic * Ibrahim Honjo

Climate Change : Time to Act

Poetry . . . Ekphrasticly Speaking

The Poetry Posse 2022

Gail Weston Shazor * Albert Carasico * Hülya N. Yılmaz
Jackie Davis Allen * Caroline Nazareno * Eliza Segiet
Alicja Maria Kuberska * Teresa E. Gallion * Joe Paire
Kimberly Burnham * Shareef Abdur – Rasheed
Ashok K. Bhargava * Elizabeth Castillo * Swapna Behera
Tezmin Ition Tsai * William S. Peters, Sr.

The Year of the Poet IX
December 2022

Featured Global Poets
Elarbi Abdelfattah * Lorraine Cragg
Neha Bhandarkar * Robert Gibbons

Climate Change Bees, Butterflies and Insect Life

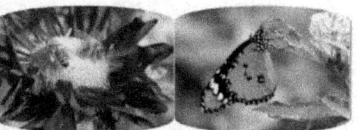

Poetry . . . Ekphrasticly Speaking

The Poetry Posse 2022

Gail Weston Shazor * Albert Carasico * Hülya N. Yılmaz
Jackie Davis Allen * Caroline Nazareno * Eliza Segiet
Alicja Maria Kuberska * Teresa E. Gallion * Joe Paire
Kimberly Burnham * Shareef Abdur – Rasheed
Ashok K. Bhargava * Elizabeth Castillo * Swapna Behera
Tezmin Ition Tsai * William S. Peters, Sr.

Now Available

www.innerchildpress.com/the-year-of-the-poet

Inner Child Press Anthologies

The Year of the Poet X
January 2023

Featured Global Poets
JuNe Barefield * Swayam Prashant
Willow Rose * Shabbirhusein K Jamnagerwalla

Children : Difference Makers

Iqbal Masih

The Poetry Posse 2023

Gail Weston Shazor * Albert Carasco * Hülya N. Yılmaz
Jackie Davis Allen * Caroline Nazareno * Kimberly Burnham
Alicja Maria Kuberska * Teresa E. Gallion * Joe Paire
Michelle Joan Barulich * Shareef Abdur – Rasheed
Ashok K. Bhargava * Elizabeth Castillo * Swapna Behera
Tezmin Ition Tsai * Eliza Segiet * William S. Peters, Sr.

The Year of the Poet X
February 2023

Featured Global Poets
Christena Williams * Hilda Graciela Kraft
Francesco Favetta * Dr. H.C. Louise Hudon

Children : Difference Makers

Ruby Bridges

The Poetry Posse 2023

Gail Weston Shazor * Albert Carasco * Hülya N. Yılmaz
Jackie Davis Allen * Caroline Nazareno * Kimberly Burnham
Alicja Maria Kuberska * Teresa E. Gallion * Joe Paire
Michelle Joan Barulich * Shareef Abdur – Rasheed
Ashok K. Bhargava * Elizabeth Castillo * Swapna Behera
Tezmin Ition Tsai * Eliza Segiet * William S. Peters, Sr.

The Year of the Poet X
March 2023

Featured Global Poets
Clarena Martinez Turizo * Binod Dawadi
Til Kumari Sharma * Petrouchka Alexieva

Children : Difference Makers

Yo Yo Ma

The Poetry Posse 2023

Gail Weston Shazor * Albert Carasco * Hülya N. Yılmaz
Jackie Davis Allen * Caroline Nazareno * Kimberly Burnham
Alicja Maria Kuberska * Teresa E. Gallion * Joe Paire
Michelle Joan Barulich * Shareef Abdur – Rasheed
Ashok K. Bhargava * Elizabeth Castillo * Swapna Behera
Tezmin Ition Tsai * Eliza Segiet * William S. Peters, Sr.

The Year of the Poet X
April 2023

Featured Global Poets
Maxwanette A Poetess * Alonzo Gross
Türkan Ergör * Ibrahim Honjo

Children : Difference Makers

Claudette Colvin

The Poetry Posse 2023

Gail Weston Shazor * Albert Carasco * Hülya N. Yılmaz
Jackie Davis Allen * Caroline Nazareno * Kimberly Burnham
Alicja Maria Kuberska * Teresa E. Gallion * Joe Paire
Michelle Joan Barulich * Shareef Abdur – Rasheed
Ashok K. Bhargava * Elizabeth Castillo * Swapna Behera
Tezmin Ition Tsai * Eliza Segiet * William S. Peters, Sr.

Now Available

www.innerchildpress.com/the-year-of-the-poet

Inner Child Press Anthologies

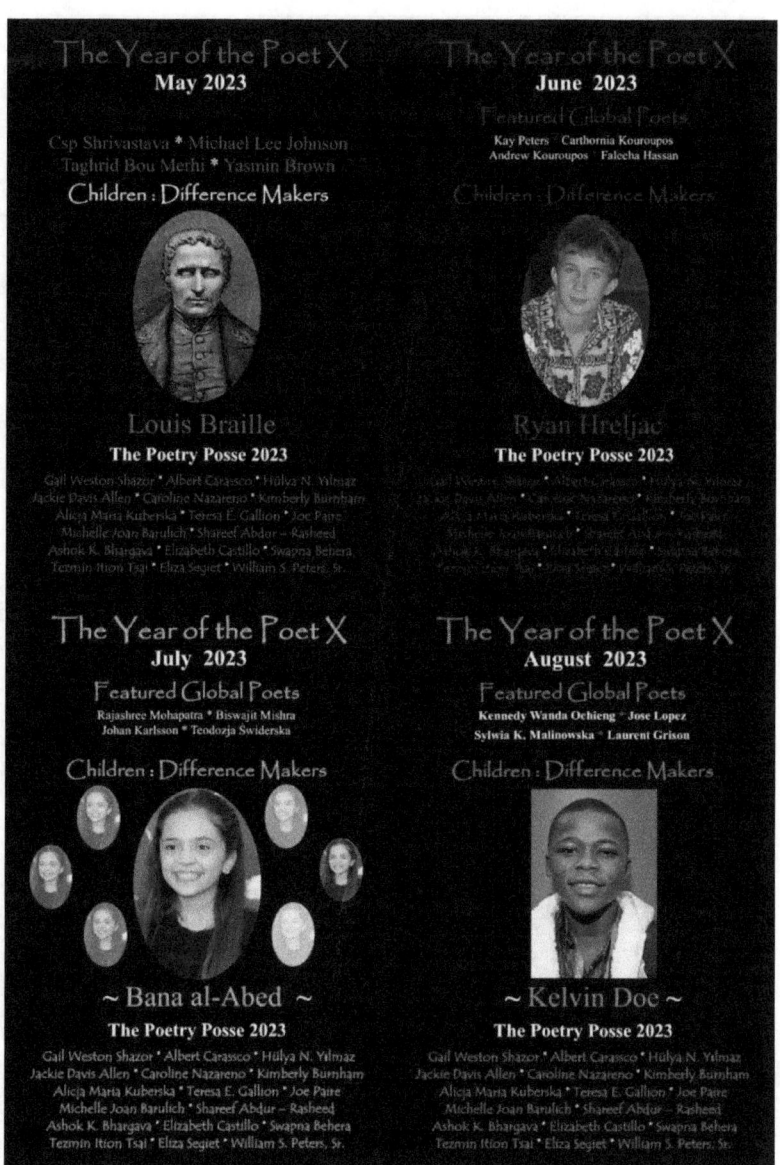

Now Available
www.innerchildpress.com/the-year-of-the-poet

Inner Child Press Anthologies

The Year of the Poet X
September 2023

Featured Global Poets
Eftichia Karpadeli * Chinh Nguyen
Nigar Agalarova * Carmela Cueva

Children : Difference Makers

~ Easton LaChappelle ~

The Poetry Posse 2023
Gail Weston Shazor * Albert Carasco * Hülya N. Yılmaz
Jackie Davis Allen * Caroline Nazareno * Kimberly Burnham
Alicja Maria Kuberska * Teresa E. Gallion * Joe Paire
Michelle Joan Barulich * Shareef Abdur – Rasheed
Ashok K. Bhargava * Elizabeth Castillo * Swapna Behera
Tezmin Ition Tsai * Eliza Segiet * William S. Peters, Sr.

The Year of the Poet X
October 2023

Featured Global Poets
CSP Shrivastava * Huniie Parker
Noreen Snyder * Ramkrishna Paul

Children : Difference Makers

~ Malala Yousafzai ~

The Poetry Posse 2023
Gail Weston Shazor * Albert Carasco * Hülya N. Yılmaz
Jackie Davis Allen * Caroline Nazareno * Kimberly Burnham
Alicja Maria Kuberska * Teresa E. Gallion * Joe Paire
Michelle Joan Barulich * Shareef Abdur – Rasheed
Ashok K. Bhargava * Elizabeth Castillo * Swapna Behera
Tezmin Ition Tsai * Eliza Segiet * William S. Peters, Sr.

The Year of the Poet X
November 2023

Featured Global Poets
Ibrahim Honjo * Balachandran Nair
Xanthi Hondrou-Hil * Francesco Favetta

Children : Difference Makers

~ Jean-Michel Basquiat ~

The Poetry Posse 2023
Gail Weston Shazor * Albert Carasco * Hülya N. Yılmaz
Jackie Davis Allen * Caroline Nazareno * Kimberly Burnham
Alicja Maria Kuberska * Teresa E. Gallion * Joe Paire
Michelle Joan Barulich * Shareef Abdur – Rasheed
Ashok K. Bhargava * Elizabeth Castillo * Swapna Behera
Tezmin Ition Tsai * Eliza Segiet * William S. Peters, Sr.

The Year of the Poet X
December 2023

Featured Global Poets
Caroline Laurent Turunc * Neha Bhandarkar
Shafkat Aziz Hajam * Elarbi Abdelfattah

Children : Difference Makers

~ Melati and Isabel Wijsen ~

The Poetry Posse 2023
Gail Weston Shazor * Albert Carasco * Hülya N. Yılmaz
Jackie Davis Allen * Caroline Nazareno * Kimberly Burnham
Alicja Maria Kuberska * Teresa E. Gallion * Joe Paire
Michelle Joan Barulich * Shareef Abdur – Rasheed
Ashok K. Bhargava * Elizabeth Castillo * Swapna Behera
Tezmin Ition Tsai * Eliza Segiet * William S. Peters, Sr.

Now Available
www.innerchildpress.com/the-year-of-the-poet

Inner Child Press Anthologies

The Year of the Poet XI
January 2024

Featured Global Poets
Til Kumari Sharma * Shafkat Aziz Hajam
Daniela Marian * Eleni Vassiliou – Asteroskon

Renowned Poets

~ Phyllis Wheatley ~

The Poetry Posse 2024

Gail Weston Shazor * Albert Carasco * Hülya N. Yılmaz
Jackie Davis Allen * Caroline Nazareno * Mutawaf Shaheed
Alicja Maria Kuberska * Teresa E. Gallion * Noreen Snyder
Michelle Joan Barulich * Shareef Abdur – Rasheed
Ashok K. Bhargava * Elizabeth Castillo * Swapna Behera
Tezmin Ition Tsai * Eliza Segiet * William S. Peters, Sr.

The Year of the Poet XI
February 2024

Featured Global Poets
Caroline Laurent Turunç * Julio Pavanetti
Lidia Chiarelli * Lina Buividavičiūtė

Renowned Poets

~ Omar Khayyam ~

The Poetry Posse 2024

Gail Weston Shazor * Albert Carasco * Hülya N. Yılmaz
Jackie Davis Allen * Caroline Nazareno * Mutawaf Shaheed
Alicja Maria Kuberska * Teresa E. Gallion * Noreen Snyder
Michelle Joan Barulich * Shareef Abdur – Rasheed
Ashok K. Bhargava * Elizabeth Castillo * Swapna Behera
Tezmin Ition Tsai * Eliza Segiet * William S. Peters, Sr.

The Year of the Poet XI
March 2024

Featured Global Poets
Francesco Favetta * Jagjit Singh Zandu
Carmela Núñez Yukimura Peruana * Michael Lee Johnson

Renowned Poets

~ Nâzim Hikmet ~

The Poetry Posse 2024

Gail Weston Shazor * Albert Carasco * Hülya N. Yılmaz
Jackie Davis Allen * Caroline Nazareno * Mutawaf Shaheed
Alicja Maria Kuberska * Teresa E. Gallion * Noreen Snyder
Michelle Joan Barulich * Shareef Abdur – Rasheed
Ashok K. Bhargava * Elizabeth Castillo * Swapna Behera
Tezmin Ition Tsai * Eliza Segiet * William S. Peters, Sr.

The Year of the Poet XI
April 2024

Featured Global Poets
Hassanal Abdullah * Johny Takkedasila
Rajashree Mohapatra * Shirley Smothers

Renowned Poets

~ William Butler Yeats ~

The Poetry Posse 2024

Gail Weston Shazor * Albert Carasco Hülya N. Yılmaz
Jackie Davis Allen * Caroline Nazareno * Mutawaf Shaheed
Alicja Maria Kuberska * Teresa E. Gallion * Noreen Snyder
Michelle Joan Barulich * Shareef Abdur – Rasheed
Ashok K. Bhargava * Elizabeth Castillo * Swapna Behera
Tezmin Ition Tsai * Eliza Segiet * William S. Peters, Sr.

Now Available

www.innerchildpress.com/the-year-of-the-poet

Inner Child Press Anthologies

The Year of the Poet XI
May 2024

Featured Global Poets
Binod Dawadi * Petros Kyriakou Veloudas
Rayees Ahmad Kumar * Solomon C Jatta

Renowned Poets

~ Makhanlal Chaturvedi ~

The Poetry Posse 2024

Gail Weston Shazor * Albert Carasco * Hülya N. Yılmaz
Jackie Davis Allen * Caroline Nazareno * Mutawaf Shaheed
Alicja Maria Kuberska * Teresa E. Gallion * Noreen Snyder
Michelle Joan Barulich * Shareef Abdur – Rasheed
Ashok K. Bhargava * Elizabeth Castillo * Swapna Behera
Tezmin Ition Tsai * Eliza Segiet * William S. Peters, Sr.

The Year of the Poet XI
June 2024

Featured Global Poets
C. S. P Shrivastava * Maria Evelyn Quilla Soleta
Moulay Cherif Chebihi Hassani * Swayam Prashant

Renowned Poets

~ Langston Hughs ~

The Poetry Posse 2024

Gail Weston Shazor * Albert Carasco * Hülya N. Yılmaz
Jackie Davis Allen * Caroline Nazareno * Mutawaf Shaheed
Alicja Maria Kuberska * Teresa E. Gallion * Noreen Snyder
Michelle Joan Barulich * Shareef Abdur – Rasheed
Ashok K. Bhargava * Elizabeth Castillo * Swapna Behera
Tezmin Ition Tsai * Eliza Segiet * William S. Peters, Sr.

The Year of the Poet XI
July 2024

Featured Global Poets
Barbara Gaiardoni * Bharati Nayak
Errol Bean * Michael Lee Johnson

Renowned Poets

~ Pablo Neruda ~

The Poetry Posse 2024

Gail Weston Shazor * Albert Carasco * Hülya N. Yılmaz
Jackie Davis Allen * Caroline Nazareno * Mutawaf Shaheed
Alicja Maria Kuberska * Teresa E. Gallion * Noreen Snyder
Michelle Joan Barulich * Shareef Abdur – Rasheed
Ashok K. Bhargava * Elizabeth Castillo * Swapna Behera
Tezmin Ition Tsai * Eliza Segiet * William S. Peters, Sr.

The Year of the Poet XI
August 2024

Featured Global Poets
Ibrahim Honjo * Khalice Jade
Irma Kurti * Mennadi Farah

Renowned Poets

~ Li Bai ~

The Poetry Posse 2024

Gail Weston Shazor * Albert Carasco * Hülya N. Yılmaz
Jackie Davis Allen * Caroline Nazareno * Mutawaf Shaheed
Alicja Maria Kuberska * Teresa E. Gallion * Noreen Snyder
Michelle Joan Barulich * Shareef Abdur – Rasheed
Ashok K. Bhargava * Elizabeth Castillo * Swapna Behera
Tezmin Ition Tsai * Eliza Segiet * William S. Peters, Sr.

Now Available

www.innerchildpress.com/the-year-of-the-poet

Inner Child Press Anthologies

The Year of the Poet XI
September 2024

Featured Global Poets
Ngozi Olivia Osuoha * Teodozja Świderska
Chinh Nguyen * Awatef El Idrissi Boukhris

Renowned Poets

~ William Ernest Henley ~
The Poetry Posse 2024

Gail Weston Shazor * Albert Carasso * Hülya N. Yılmaz
Jackie Davis Allen * Caroline Nazareno * Mutawaf Shaheed
Alicja Maria Kuberska * Teresa E. Gallion * Noreen Snyder
Michelle Joan Barulich * Shareef Abdur – Rasheed
Ashok K. Bhargava * Elizabeth Castillo * Swapna Behera
Tezmin Ition Tsai * Eliza Segiet * William S. Peters, Sr.

The Year of the Poet XI
October 2024

Featured Global Poets
Deepak Kumar Dey * Shallal 'Anouz
Adnan Al-Sayegh * Taghrid Bou Merhi

Renowned Poets

~ Adam Mickiewicz ~
The Poetry Posse 2024

Gail Weston Shazor * Albert Carasso * Hülya N. Yılmaz
Jackie Davis Allen * Caroline Nazareno * Mutawaf Shaheed
Alicja Maria Kuberska * Teresa E. Gallion * Noreen Snyder
Michelle Joan Barulich * Shareef Abdur – Rasheed
Ashok K. Bhargava * Elizabeth Castillo * Swapna Behera
Tezmin Ition Tsai * Eliza Segiet * William S. Peters, Sr.

The Year of the Poet XI
November 2024

Featured Global Poets
Abraham Tawiah Tei * Neha Bhandarkar
Zaneta Varnado Johns * Haseena Bnaiyan

Renowned Poets

~ Wole Soyinka ~
The Poetry Posse 2024

Gail Weston Shazor * Albert Carasso * Hülya N. Yılmaz
Jackie Davis Allen * Caroline Nazareno * Mutawaf Shaheed
Alicja Maria Kuberska * Teresa E. Gallion * Noreen Snyder
Michelle Joan Barulich * Shareef Abdur – Rasheed
Ashok K. Bhargava * Elizabeth Castillo * Swapna Behera
Tezmin Ition Tsai * Eliza Segiet * William S. Peters, Sr.

The Year of the Poet XI
December 2024

Featured Global Poets
Kapardeli Eftichia * Irena Jovanović
Sudipta Mishra * Til Kumari Sharma

Renowned Poets

~ Imru' al-Qais ~
The Poetry Posse 2024

Gail Weston Shazor * Albert Carasso * Hülya N. Yılmaz
Jackie Davis Allen * Caroline Nazareno * Mutawaf Shaheed
Alicja Maria Kuberska * Teresa E. Gallion * Noreen Snyder
Michelle Joan Barulich * Shareef Abdur – Rasheed * Swapna Behera
Ashok K. Bhargava * Elizabeth Castillo * Kimberly Burnham
Tezmin Ition Tsai * Eliza Segiet * William S. Peters, Sr.

Now Available
www.innerchildpress.com/the-year-of-the-poet

Inner Child Press Anthologies

The Year of the Poet XII
January 2025

Featured Global Poets

Khalice Jade * Til Kumari Sharma
Sushant Thapa * Orbindu Ganga

 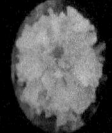 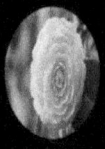

Innocence   Joy   Longing
Daisy   Marigold   Camellia

The Poetry Posse 2025

Gail Weston Shazor * Albert Carasso * Hülya N. Yılmaz
Jackie Davis Allen * Caroline Nazareno * Mutawaf Shaheed
Alicja Maria Kuberska * Teresa E. Gallion * Noreen Snyder
Shareef Abdur – Rasheed * Swapna Behera * Eliza Segiet
Ashok K. Bhargava * Elizabeth Castillo * Kimberly Burnham
Tzemin Ition Tsai * William S. Peters, Sr.

The Year of the Poet XII
February 2025

Featured Global Poets

Shafkat Aziz Hajam * Frosina Tasevska
Muhammad Gaddafi Masoud * Karen Morrison

 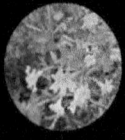 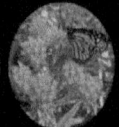

Curiosity   Fear   Lonliness
Hibiscus   Minulus   Butterfly Weed

The Poetry Posse 2025

Gail Weston Shazor * Albert Carasso * Hülya N. Yılmaz
Jackie Davis Allen * Caroline Nazareno * Mutawaf Shaheed
Alicja Maria Kuberska * Teresa E. Gallion * Noreen Snyder
Shareef Abdur – Rasheed * Swapna Behera * Eliza Segiet
Ashok K. Bhargava * Elizabeth Castillo * Kimberly Burnham
Tzemin Ition Tsai * William S. Peters, Sr.

The Year of the Poet XII
March 2025

Featured Global Poets

Deepak Kumar Dey * Binod Dawadi
Faleeha Hassan * Kapardeli Eftichia

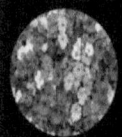 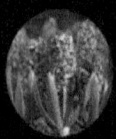 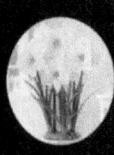

Frustration   Sorrow   Detrmination
Petunias   Purple Hyacinth   Amaryllis

The Poetry Posse 2025

Gail Weston Shazor * Albert Carasso * Hülya N. Yılmaz
Jackie Davis Allen * Caroline Nazareno * Mutawaf Shaheed
Alicja Maria Kuberska * Teresa E. Gallion * Noreen Snyder
Shareef Abdur – Rasheed * Swapna Behera * Eliza Segiet
Ashok K. Bhargava * Elizabeth Castillo * Kimberly Burnham
Tzemin Ition Tsai * William S. Peters, Sr.

The Year of the Poet XII
April 2025

Featured Global Poets

Gopal Sinha * Taghrid Bou Merhi
Irma Kurti * Marlon Salem Gruezo

  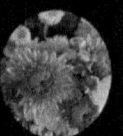

Resilience   Self Doubt   Grief
Calendula   Centaury   Chrysanthemums

The Poetry Posse 2025

Gail Weston Shazor * Albert Carasso * Hülya N. Yılmaz
Jackie Davis Allen * Caroline Nazareno * Mutawaf Shaheed
Alicja Maria Kuberska * Teresa E. Gallion * Noreen Snyder
Shareef Abdur – Rasheed * Swapna Behera * Eliza Segiet
Ashok K. Bhargava * Elizabeth Castillo * Kimberly Burnham
Tzemin Ition Tsai * William S. Peters, Sr.

Now Available

www.innerchildpress.com/the-year-of-the-poet

and there is much, much more !

visit . . .

www.innerchildpress.com/anthologies-sales-special.php

Also check out our Authors and all the wonderful Books Available at :

www.innerchildpress.com/authors-pages

Inner Child Press Anthologies

Now Available

www.worldhealingworldpeacepoetry.com

Inner Child Press Anthologies

Now Available

www.worldhealingworldpeacepoetry.com

Inner Child Press Anthologies

Now Available

www.worldhealingworldpeacepoetry.com

Inner Child Press Anthologies

Now Available

www.worldhealingworldpeacepoetry.com

World Healing World Peace
2012, 2014, 2016, 2018, 2020, 2022, 2024

Now Available

www.worldhealingworldpeacepoetry.com

Inner Child Press International

'building bridges of cultural understanding'

Meet the Board of Directors

William S. Peters, Sr.
Chair Person
Founder
Inner Child Enterprises
Inner Child Press

Hülya N Yılmaz
Director
Editing Services
Co-Chair Person

Fahredin B. Shehu
Director
Cultural Affairs

Elizabeth E. Castillo
Director
Recording Secretary

De'Andre Hawthorne
Director
Performance Poetry

Gail Weston Shazor
Director
Anthologies

Kimberly Burnham
Director
Cultural Ambassador
Pacific Northwest
USA

Ashok K. Bhargava
Director
WIN Awards

Deborah Smart
Director
Publicity
Marketing

www.innerchildpress.com

Inner Child Press International

'building bridges of cultural understanding'

Meet our Cultural Ambassadors

Fahredia Shehu
Director of Cultural

Faleha Hassan
Iraq – USA

Elizabeth E. Castillo
Philippines

Antoinette Coleman
Chicago
Midwest USA

Ananda Nepali
Nepal – Tibet
Northern India

Kimberly Burnham
Pacific Southwest
USA

Alicja Kuberska
Poland
Eastern Europe

Swapna Behera
India
Southeast Asia

Kolade O. Freedom
Nigeria
West Africa

Monsif Beroual
Morocco
Northern Africa

Ashok K. Bhargava
Canada

Tzemin Ition Tsai
Republic of China
Greater China

Alicia M. Ramirez
Mexico
Central America

Christena AV Williams
Jamaica
Caribbean

Louise Hudon
Eastern Canada

Aziz Mountassir
Morocco
Northern Africa

Shareef Abdur-Rasheed
Southeastern USA

Laure Charazac
France
Western Europe

Mohammad Ikbal Harb
Lebanon
Middle East

Mohamed Abdel
Aziz Shmeis
Egypt
Middle East

Hilary Maiinga
Kenya
Eastern Africa

Josephus R. Johnson
Liberia

Mennadi Farah
Algeria

www.innerchildpress.com

This Anthological Publication
is underwritten solely by

Inner Child Press International

Inner Child Press is a Publishing Company Founded and Operated by Writers. Our personal publishing experiences provides us an intimate understanding of the sometimes daunting challenges Writers, New and Seasoned may face in the Business of Publishing and Marketing their Creative "Written Work".

For more Information

Inner Child Press International

www.innerchildpress.com

'building bridges of cultural understanding'
202 Wiltree Court, State College, Pennsylvania 16801

www.innerchildpress.com

~ fini ~

www.ingramcontent.com/pod-product-compliance
Lightning Source LLC
LaVergne TN
LVHW051042080426
835508LV00019B/1652